THREE PROFESSIONAL MEN

REVEAL HOW TO GET

MR. RIGHT TO POP THE QUESTION

Marry Me!

BRADLEY GERSTMAN, ESQ.

CHRISTOPHER PIZZO, C.P.A.

RICH SELDES, M.D.

Cliff Street Books

An Imprint of HarperCollins*Publishers*

HarperCollins books may be purchased for educational, business, or sales promotional use. For information please write: Special Markets Department, HarperCollins Publishers Inc., 10 East 53rd Street, New York, NY 10022.

FIRST EDITION

Designed by William Ruoto

Printed on acid-free paper

Library of Congress Cataloging-in-Publication Data

Gerstman, Bradley.
    Marry me! : three professional men reveal how to get Mr. Right to
pop the question / Bradley Gerstman, Christopher Pizzo, Rich Seldes.
        p. cm.
    ISBN 0-06-019539-8
    1. Dating (Social customs)   2. Man-woman relationships.
3. Marriage.   I. Pizzo, Christopher. II. Seldes, Rich.   III. Title.

HQ801 .G4 2000
306.73—dc21   00-040469

00 01 02 03 04 ❖/RRD 10 9 8 7 6 5 4 3 2 1

To my beautiful wife, Cheryl

—Bradley Gerstman

To my mother, Barbara, and my father, George, for all
of your continued inspiration and support

—Chris Pizzo

To Marla, the most beautiful woman in the world, who
has made me the happiest man in the world

—Rich Seldes

CONTENTS

ACKNOWLEDGMENTS

I would like to thank my parents, my sister, Linda, my brother, Danny, and his wife, Pam, for all the love and support they have given me along the way; and my late sister, Lisa, whose light reaches me still. I also extend a special thanks to my wife, Cheryl, whom I love more and more each day.

—*Bradley Gerstman*

I thank my mom, Barbara, and dad, George, for all the help along the way. Thank you to my grandparents, Sue and Sal—you and your marriage of sixty-one years remain my inspiration for happily-ever-after.

—*Chris Pizzo*

I would like to thank Marla, Mom, Dad, and Grandma for your love and continuous support. Special thanks to Ruth, Dan, and Stu for making me feel like one of the family.

—*Rich Seldes*

All three of us would like to thank Amelia Sheldon for helping us put our thoughts into words. Stedman Mays and Mary Tahan at Clausen, Mays & Tahan Literary Agency have our gratitude for their continuing hard work and good humor.

We couldn't ask for a more intelligent, understanding, or dedicated agent than Stedman, who has spent countless hours wisely and patiently guiding us through the writing and publishing process twice now. We will always be indebted to our editor, Diane Reverand, for her unerring eye, ingenious suggestions, and enthusiastic support. We are grateful for the concerted efforts of Janet Dery, Jennifer Suitor, and everyone else at Cliff Street, HarperCollins, and HarperAudio for helping us bring this book into existence. We extend a big thank-you to all of our readers whose questions and support in e-mails, letters, and at book signings for *What Men Want* inspired this second book. And, of course, we are forever thankful for the late Connie Clausen who gave us our start and whose spirit inspires us still.

1
—

INSIDE THE MIND AND HEART OF THE COMMITTED MAN

Yes, it's true. We used to be swinging single men—out on the town every night, meeting women, partying like crazy, dating up a storm. But, now, two of us have actually settled down in a committed relationship (and one is looking to do the same). Wondering what it took for us professional men to say good-bye to bachelorhood and actually pop the question? Well, we're about to tell you.

But first let us tell you who we are. We're three professional guys who helped women friends with their dating questions and found that our advice actually worked. Drawing from our own experiences, we spoke frankly about how we think and react in relationships. As it turned out, our insight was new to the women with whom we shared it, and our advice was helpful to them in their romantic dealings with men. Over time, we recognized that most guys held

similar views about relationships. So, with the encouragement of our friends, we decided to write a book to help
women understand men.

Our first book, *What Men Want—Three Professional Single Men Reveal to Women What It Takes to Make a Man Yours*,
was very well received worldwide. Here in the United States,
we were interviewed on television shows including *The View,
20/20, The Charles Grodin Show, Montel Williams*, and *Ger-
aldo*. We appeared on such national radio shows as the *Tom
Leykis Show* and *Loveline*. We were even a *Cosmopolitan* magazine cover story. *What Men Want* was translated into more
than a dozen languages and warmly embraced by women all
over the world. Our Web site, www.whatmenwant.com, continues to attract thousands of visitors.

Since the publication of *What Men Want* two years ago,
we've received thousands of letters and e-mails from our
readers around the world telling us how we've helped them
understand men. How we've saved their relationships. How
they appreciate our straightforward, honest, and friendly
tone. To this day, our first book remains a dating bible for
thousands of women.

But women want more answers from us. How do we
know? In addition to fan mail, we've also received hundreds
of letters from readers asking additional questions about
men, dating, and marriage. What's the most common question that women ask us? "Why are men afraid of commitment?" We are flooded with letters from women who want
to get married, but can't seem to overcome their boyfriends'
fear of commitment. We've been asked about this issue so
much, in fact, that we decided to devote a whole book to it.

So, *Marry Me! Three Professional Men Reveal How to Get
Mr. Right to Pop the Question* is our "Popping the Question"
bible. In it we expose the way men feel about commitment—

including all the dirty details. In response to what we know about men's fear of the "C" word, we include here a four-step program to help you avoid the typical roadblocks to commitment and become the kind of girl he'll classify as "marriage material." (And like it or not, men do sit around talking to each other about how this woman is "marriage material," and that woman isn't—this woman has "wife potential," and that woman doesn't.) We spilled our guts in *What Men Want*—we disclosed men's deepest, darkest feelings, and we're back to do it again. Now we are focusing specifically on men's approach to committed intimacy. We hope what we have to share will help you bring that special man down the aisle next to you.

Some relationship authors think that all you need to land a man is a frivolous code, or to accept the fact that your man retreats into a cave, or some old-fashioned rules that worked for your grandmother. We think it's a bit deeper than that. And we want to share with you the truth about how the male mind really works. Why should you listen to us? We are three guys who represent the full spectrum of men heading toward marital commitment. Chris is single and searching, Rich is engaged, and Brad is married. These different profiles enable us to offer a wide range of experiences, insights, and perspectives on the male approach to commitment. We bet you're wondering how in the world Brad, the player among us, got snagged. No one believed it was possible—not Chris, Rich, or any of our friends. This is proof that it *can* happen to any guy. Getting a guy to commit to marriage is not impossible. We will show you how and why Brad and Rich popped the question. You'll soon see that all it takes is the right woman who follows the proper steps.

When it comes to answering relationship questions men's lips are generally sealed shut. As you know, men rarely feel comfortable revealing their inner emotions and thoughts. When it comes to matters of the heart, it's as if they can't even speak. But as we've said all along, behind that tough exterior is a very vulnerable, caring man. In this book we will share:

- Why men can commit to their careers—but not to a relationship
- What men think about dating divorced women and single mothers
- What's really going on inside men's heads when you start to get serious
- How sex changes once you're in a committed relationship
- How men truly feel about moving in together
- The specific psychological stages a man goes through as he approaches commitment
- The steps you can take to reassure a man who is about to pop the question

We are three professional men—Brad is a lawyer, Chris is an accountant, and Rich is a doctor—and our book gives you a private peek into the hearts and minds of professional men. We don't hold anything back. We tell you exactly how it is. Being lifelong friends, we three are able to be completely honest with one another and to discuss the topics that most men avoid—their inner thoughts, their emotions, and their true feelings about love and relationships. We are able to compare our thoughts and provide solid insight into how the professional single man—or any man serious about pursuing a career—views commitment, engagement, and marriage. We share our experiences, our feelings, and our advice. Having consulted with other men all over the country, we are amazed at how their fears, emotions, needs, and relationship patterns are so similar to ours, whether they're professionals or blue-collar workers. This has only confirmed for us that—even with career, economic, or geographical differences—when it comes right down to it, men consistently share a very similar perspective.

Our approach? Think of us as your best guy friends. Picture us talking to you in a bar or lounge. You've been feeling completely baffled and befuddled by men and what they want. You turn to us and ask us questions—about men, their motives, and their feelings on committed relationships. Well, friends, here are the answers you've been waiting for. You see, it's simple for the three of us to answer your questions because we know how men think. Our straightforward, relaxed approach might shock you—or it might put you at ease. Either way, we will unveil for you the secrets of how your boyfriend can be transformed into the perfect husband.

This book is for all engaged, dating, and single women. We realize that women want to understand how men think—how they view marriage, and each specific step leading up to it. We'll help you do just that by surveying the type of relationship in which you're currently involved. Is it simply a "good for now" relationship? If it is, you must realize that your man will never marry you. Does your relationship have the potential to move to the ultimate level of lifelong commitment? Then we'll tell you how to become a woman with "wife potential"—a girl who's "marriage material" in men's eyes, what we call a "marriage material" girl—by providing you with the essential how-to's to get your boyfriend to tie the knot. With our help your odds of marrying Mr. Right are much higher.

Since the publication of *What Men Want,* each of us has gained even further insight into relationships. We know firsthand what keeps men from moving toward commitment. And we are ready to share it all. But first, we'll fill you in on where we've been and what we've been up to lately:

BRAD: A great deal has changed for Brad. Brad used to be the "player" among us. He is a sharp-dressing, headstrong type who loves to debate. In college, he played football, won a student athlete award, and made the dean's list. After practicing law as an Assistant District Attorney in the Bronx, Brad started his own law firm. Before he met Cheryl he played the field and had a few serious relationships. But then Cheryl came along. Cheryl intuitively knew how to nurture Brad through his male obstacles to commitment and popping the question. Since *What Men Want* was first published, Brad dated, proposed to, and married Cheryl. She's everything in the world to Brad. The two of them are happily married and reside in New York City. Brad finds married life exciting and rewarding. He enjoys spending all of his free time with Cheryl—they love going to the gym, eating out, and visiting family. As far as work is concerned, Brad has transitioned from partner in a law firm to general counsel in a New York corporation.

CHRIS: Chris remains the "romantic" among us. Against all odds, Chris has achieved a lot. After being raised by a single mother on a limited budget, Chris was determined to succeed. After college, he passed the C.P.A. exam, completed his M.B.A., went on to work at a Big Five accounting firm, started two Internet companies, and is now an entrepreneurial business consultant. In college, Chris played football and fell in love during his senior year. When that relationship ended four years later, he put a

Band-Aid on his heart and started looking for Ms. Right. He has been actively looking ever since. Chris's open-heartedness sometimes leaves him feeling too vulnerable to the hurts inflicted by others, but his affectionate nature and direct style win him the friendship of many who know him. Chris represents the single man among us. Still in the throes of dating, Chris can relate firsthand to the trials and tribulations of what men—and women—go through. Though he remains very focused on his career, he is still on the lookout for Ms. Right.

RICH: We think of Rich as the "intellectual" among us. He is cultured, well traveled, and appreciates the finer things in life. As president of his college fraternity, member of his college football team, and summa cum laude graduate, Rich has always led by example. He went on to medical school to become a doctor. As a surgeon and a man, Rich proceeds with a measured pace and a steady hand. In medical school and as a physician, he needed—and had trouble finding—a woman who gave him the space and time to pursue his career. After years of dating women who played games, he finally met Marla.

Since *What Men Want,* Rich and Marla have moved in together and are now engaged. Rich learned how to share his life with another person. He has experienced balancing his busy lifestyle as a doctor with being a dedicated fiancé. He went through the nervousness that comes along with moving in with a girlfriend and the anxiety of buying an engagement ring. He has also experienced the pleasure that comes with proposing to the woman he loves, and watching her smile and say, "Yes, I will marry you!" Rich and Marla are happily living together in New York and are excited about their upcoming wedding. Rich is an orthopedic surgeon at North Star Orthopedics in Forest Hills, New York.

So, that's who we are—three guys representing the full spectrum of searching for, becoming engaged to, and marrying Ms. Right. As you can see, we aren't so-called experts from the outside looking in at the world of dating and commitment. We have lived our experience and that's why so many female readers trust what we have to say. We don't like to see women stuck in dead-end relationships forever with their hopes and dreams of marriage never realized. We want to help.

After reading *Marry Me!* you will know how to nurture Mr. Right so he will feel comfortable committing to you, getting engaged, and then married. You will feel as if you finally have had that conversation your boyfriend has continuously avoided. We'll tell you the things you do that drive men away. And what it is that most women don't do, but can do, with a little guidance, to capture men's hearts. We'll explain what it takes for you to be filed under the heading "marriage material" in the mental filing cabinet of Mr. Right. We have the essential information for you to prepare a man to let go of the single life, commit to a woman, get engaged, and most important, get married!

Now that you know what's in store, we thought we'd start off by letting you in on some basic facts about men and commitment.

2

—

TEN FACTS ABOUT COMMITMENT

These ten facts may be harsh, but we promise they'll help you better understand men. The road to marriage has many obstacles, and we want to help you get there as easily as possible. With these facts under your belt, you will have more power to get your man exactly where you want him—down that aisle and happily married!

FACT NUMBER 1

Women Have the Power to Make a Man Commit

Women have more power to make a man commit to monogamy and to marriage than they realize. In fact, when it comes to commitment, women hold all the power. That's because men are afraid of commitment and a man acting from fear is not a man in power. True love gives men the first glimpse of a time when there will be no more sex with other women. This change is scary for a man and he must work through his fears before he moves toward monogamy and marriage. But don't worry. Even the biggest players in the world are capable of committing to a long-term relationship—just look at Brad! But you must realize that as the special woman he loves, you are the only one who can give your man the time he needs to change his focus from short-term dating fun to long-term feelings and commitment.

When a woman treats a relationship that is growing serious with confidence and faith instead of uncertainty and demands, she gives her guy the kind of reassurance he needs to move forward even if he is petrified. To help you get your man through this tricky period we've devised the foolproof Engagement Formula and share it in Chapter 8. If you read on and follow our advice on how to get him to propose, before you know it you'll be his one and only love.

FACT NUMBER 2

Engagement Is Not About Timing

It's about being the right woman—and taking the right steps. Men sense that women have a deadline, time line, or certain age by which they feel they must be engaged. The truth is that men don't feel the pressure of a deadline for themselves—or for women. "Time limit" thinking is counterproductive to a good relationship. Women should throw away their rigid relationship calendars and instead let things develop naturally. A romantic relationship is not a work project and should not have a strict deadline. To be honest, trying to meet an arbitrary deadline will only put pressure on the professional man. Since guys like us deal with deadlines so often in our careers, the last thing we want is another one in our relationships. If your man feels you pushing a commitment on him, he'll want to run for the hills.

If you feel disappointed because you won't be engaged to the man of your dreams after dating for a year, or married to him by thirty, just think how far behind you'd be if Mr. Right broke up with you. That is just what could happen if you try to rush commitment or engagement. If you put the heat on, you ultimately alienate the man in your life, because he starts either to see you as desperate or to sense that something must be wrong between the two of you. Why else would you be in such a big rush? he wonders.

If everything is progressing nicely, missing an arbitrary deadline would be a poor reason for letting a good guy go. Don't scare your man away by saying "time is running out." If you are confident your man sees you as a woman with wife potential, let him make the marriage proposal when he is ready.

FACT NUMBER 3

A Professional Man Has Three Distinct Stages of His Career

Professional men go through three stages in their careers— the Not-Yet-Set Stage, the Transition Stage, and the Successful Stage. At each stage, men have different needs and desires.

During the Not-Yet-Set Stage a man struggles to establish

himself in his competitive career track. A related part of the Not-Yet-Set Stage is the Comeback/Starting-Over Stage. This is the phase of a man's work life when he's recently changed careers, gotten fired or laid off, or is having a hard time finding a job.

In the second stage, the Transition Stage, a man has defined an industry and a career path that he finds fulfilling. He is positioning himself to perform well, really reach for the stars, and become a great success one day. The Transition Stage of a man's career is characterized by a marked increase in his confidence and sense of direction.

In the Successful Stage men are comfortable in their professions. They are financially stable and respected. They are confident about their ability to achieve their goals. In addition, men at this stage are also more focused on friends and family. They have established a strong track record and are confident that they will be successful at almost anything they do.

FACT NUMBER 4

To Understand a Man, a Woman Must Understand His Career— and His Career Stage

A professional man's relationship will be enhanced if his career prospers, and his career will prosper if his relationship with the special woman in his life is sailing smoothly. If you have a career of your own, you are probably familiar with the challenges a man faces on a demanding career track and how a strong relationship can support a climb up the ladder of success. But what you may be hesitant to embrace is the fact that a man's job is first and foremost before anything in his mind—before your relationship and before your job.

A man's entire identity is tied to his success, and a man's job is still the measure of his success in his own eyes and the eyes of society. A woman can be seen as a brilliant business woman and/or a supportive wife and mother. The day a good father is as well respected as a successful professional man will be a great one, but it hasn't come yet. For a professional man to feel complete, he must be successful and be gratified at work.

By understanding your man's career and the particular stage he is at, you can get a much better grasp on your relationship with him. If you know what a man is looking for and what he is able to give to a relationship at each stage of his career, you will be able to decide whether a relationship with him is worth pursuing. You will be able to make a clear-cut decision as to whether you are willing and able to give your man what he needs and take from him what he is able to give at that particular stage. With this knowledge, you will be able to complement your man as he grows in his career and together you will be able to foster a happy, healthy, progressive relationship that will eventually lead to engagement and marriage.

FACT NUMBER 5

A Professional Man's Level of Commitment Is Directly Related to the Career Stage He Is In

Why isn't your man committing to your relationship? Perhaps you're not responding properly to the career stage that he is in. Here are the signs that will help you recognize where your man is:

Not-Yet-Set Stage: During this time, a man may love to date and meet women, but he often isn't hunting for a long-term relationship. As a man focuses on building his career, he often feels uncertain about his future and commonly doubts his ability to succeed. He usually works long hours to learn his field and to make a good impression on his supervisors. Having not yet established himself in his career, the professional man in the Not-Yet-Set Stage is often confronting many of his own insecurities. If the right woman comes along a commitment is definitely possible, but she will most likely have to have enough confidence in the relationship for two.

When a man is in the similar Comeback/Starting-Over Stage, he is feeling either the stress of a big challenge or down in the dumps because he has had to start at "go" all over again. Whether he has just had a big promotion or a lay-off, a man at this juncture is often putting most of his energy into work. He needs a girlfriend who will listen to him, provide positive reinforcement, comfort him, and give him space to work through his own fears and outside pressures until he proves himself in a new situation or lands on his feet after a setback. The good news? A man will forever remember that you helped him through the tough times.

Transition Stage: When a professional man is in the Transition Stage—making the jump from an entry-level to a more established position in the hierarchy of his chosen field—he will focus completely on making this move successfully. As he sees it, the doctor, lawyer, or accountant must deliver now if he is to advance any farther in his career. With all of his future plans and dreams resting on his ability to shine at this moment, the professional man will do virtually anything to meet the new requirements he faces. In fact, it is not uncommon for a man at this stage to put his relationship on hold—at least until he feels settled in his new work role and more comfortable with its added responsibilities. If the frequency of dates and calls from your man falls off or lapses completely during this period, don't worry. Take your man's distance as a response to career demands and not the sign of an ailing relationship. Once his career really starts taking off, your relationship—and his commitment to it—is likely to hit its stride, too.

Successful Stage: When a man is in the Successful Stage of his career he is feeling confident and settled at work. He is usually in a high position and pulling down a healthy salary. As a result, his focus often turns toward establishing a long-term commitment with a woman. He may even be thinking about marriage and a family before he finds Ms. Right. When a man in the Successful Stage meets a woman with whom he feels very comfortable, he might not hesitate to move the relationship along quickly. At this point in his career, he wants to share what he has with someone special and often has the time to build a satisfying relationship with the right woman.

FACT NUMBER 6

There Are Things a Woman Can Do to Bring the Relationship to a Higher Level—Tips Custom-made for Each Career Stage

In order to commit to a long-term relationship with a woman, a man needs particular things. Give him what he needs for the career stage he is at and—believe it or not—he may be the one bringing up commitment. Want to help your man and nurture a strong and healthy relationship through each stage? Here's how:

Not-Yet-Set Stage: First and foremost, men in this stage need continuous votes of confidence, moral support, and positive reinforcement. A man at this stage of his career also likes the woman he loves to take an interest in his new venture. Plan fun activities to get his mind off work every now and then. He will greatly appreciate your thoughtfulness and effort.

Transition Stage: Above all, a man in the Transition Stage must have the time and space he requests from you to focus on work. If you want to keep him, don't make your man feel guilty about not spending more time with you or bring up serious relationship issues at this stage. Don't pressure a man into marrying you while he is in the transition phase. He will likely respond by ending the relationship.

Successful Stage: A woman's true focus on a man *for himself* is of the utmost importance if she wants to land him in this stage of his career. Successful men are ready to discuss your relationship and some of the deeper issues that come with it much sooner than you will expect. A man at this stage wants to know a woman is with him for who he is not for what he can buy her. If your man has any reason to think that you are a gold digger, he will be gone faster than you can say, "Diamonds are a girl's best friend."

FACT NUMBER 7

A Man's Success in His Career
Is an Accomplishment for the Man
and His Girlfriend

Professional men aren't slaving away at their jobs just for themselves—they're doing it for their women, too. Of course, a man takes a particularly strong sense of pride in his own accomplishments, but there's another kind of pride he feels when he is able to share this success with the woman he loves. Whether it's about being the breadwinner, the caretaker, the provider, the man of the house, the captain of the team or just plain hero, a man gets a rush when his girlfriend is there offering support for his hard work and sharing in his happiness as he reaches important career goals. A man wants to feel as if his girlfriend is on his team—through thick and thin. That's why when he kicks butt in his career, she should sincerely feel that he's done it for her—as well as for himself. A man has the desire to be a provider for his wife and family—even if his wife has a career. He must feel that he is providing for you, which makes him feel fulfilled and happy. The more he loves you, the more he will want to provide for you and be successful at work.

FACT NUMBER 8

For a Man, Living Together Before
Engagement Is a Requirement

If both you and your man are comfortable about living together before marriage, then we strongly suggest that you move in with one another. Living together brings your relationship to another level that cannot be achieved if you continue to live separately. The first weeks or months of living together are a learning period, really a crash course, on how to get along with your romantic partner in spite of all of his unique foibles and habits. Don't worry if there's a little friction at first. Cohabitation allows you to work out most of the rough edges and bumps that come with living under one roof before you make that final commitment to each other. Now you can get used to seeing him eating ice cream out of the carton, and he can come to know you in that bright green avocado mask that keeps your skin so clear. Though irritating or downright frightening at first, these shared experiences actually can become endearing after a few weeks.

Now let's get to the real reasons why we feel it is mandatory for a man to live with you before popping the question. Living together provides another stage, another allotment of time, during which men start thinking about spending their lives and sharing their beds with just one woman. Waking up next to you on a regular basis helps convince Mr. Right that this is really what he does want for the rest of his life. He sees that sex can still be good even when you don't rush off to separate lives in the morning. He realizes that there is maybe even more sex when you don't have to arrange to be at the same place when the lights go out. Then, there are other perks such as more home-cooked meals, shared showers, and just your winning smile when he gets home after a hard day at the office. Ultimately, living together quells men's fears about monogamy for life by bringing the upside home for them, day after day.

FACT NUMBER 9

Moving in with a Woman
Is Not Easy for a Man

Although moving in with a woman is preferred on his road to engagement and marriage, in no way is it easy for a man. Having a new female roommate actually complicates his life quite a bit, driving his anxiety level sky high. The professional man has most likely grown very comfortable in his bachelor lifestyle and has enjoyed the ultimate in independence—never having to answer to anyone. He has been able to sit on the couch naked all day, watching sports, and even farting loudly if he wants to. He has been able to leave the toilet seat up all the time. He has been able to store dishes in the sink for weeks and never clean the bathtub. When a man moves in with a woman, he has to change his comfortable routine. He also essentially gives up any chance of dating other women. He has to throw his black book away. When a man makes the decision to move in with a woman, he gives up a huge chunk of his independence for her. She has to be special enough for him to do so. Don't buy those arguments you will hear about your guy not wanting to marry you if he can just live with you. Only a woman whom he would want to marry would qualify for this extreme life change.

FACT NUMBER 10

He Will Love You More and Want to Marry You Sooner if You Don't Give Him Ultimatums or Pressure Him into Marriage

If you want to see your man sprint away from you as if you were a charging bull, then give him an ultimatum on marriage. The worst thing you can do is to force him into a corner and tell him to either commit to marrying you or else. You will *never* force him to marry you. If you press the issue with Mr. Right, he will drop the idea completely, even if he was seriously considering asking you to be his wife just moments before. Men don't respond well to power plays—or time limits—especially when it comes to relationships. If you give your man an ultimatum, he will think that you are trying to control him. Envisioning a girlfriend as a soon-to-be controlling wife is the biggest turnoff a man can imagine. Trust us on this one.

If a man has told you that he loves you and wants to be with you, that's great news. If he backs up this statement by spending time with you and including you in his life, you are in a loving relationship. If this describes your situation, you should not jeopardize what you have by pushing and nagging him to get married. Enjoy your relationship and have faith that it is heading in the right direction. Have confidence that your man will come to propose when he is comfortable with the idea and the time is right for him. Marriage is one of the most important decisions a man will make. If he is forced to make the decision before he is ready, then he will back out quickly. *He will love you more and want to marry you sooner if you don't give him ultimatums or pressure him into marriage.*

*   *   *

These are some basic facts about men and commitment. In the pages that follow, we will divulge what goes on inside a man as he contemplates popping the question. We'll reveal dating secrets from the male perspective, and we'll advise you on how to move from "wife-potential" to wife. And of course, we'll talk about sex (did you think we'd leave that out?) and give answers to the most commonly asked questions we've received from readers in letters and e-mails. Last, we'll fill you in on a man's experiences during the engagement period. Once you see how simple it is to get a man to commit, your relationship anxiety will disappear, and you can begin to enjoy your healthy, happy committed relationship. You will better understand your man—and turn him from uncommitted boyfriend into loving husband.

3

THE NUMBER-ONE COMMITMENT KEY: UNDERSTANDING A MAN'S CAREER PATH

Does a man you're dating have all the actions and words of Mr. Right but seem to be stuck in a rut of not really committing himself to you? Do you believe that your monogamous boyfriend should be moving your relationship along a little faster by popping the question already? Are you concerned that he hasn't pegged you as a woman with "wife potential," that you're not the "marriage material" girl he wants to take to the altar? Well, you may have a huge blind spot when it comes to your man and his ability to commit to you. He may see a huge roadblock to greater commitment that you haven't considered. Don't worry, we're not going to tell you that he's gay. Your guy's job may be coming between you and the ring.

You read this right. Your guy doesn't look at The Relationship first, as you might. A man's career is the single most important factor he will consider when deciding whether to take his relationship to the next level. Like it or not, a man's career comes before everything else in his life, even love. A man knows that it is through his singular ability to excel in his career that he receives deep personal gratification, the ability to support a wife and family, and the respect of those around him.

We've identified three different career stages for men and how each of these distinctly affects his relationships. In this chapter, we will tell you how to identify your man's career stage, and what you can do to maximize your chances of his committing to marry you in each one.

Men and Their Careers

A man's career is of the utmost importance to him. In some cases, men become completely focused on their professions and their desire to excel in them, losing sight of everything else life has to offer. Can you blame us? We feel most comfortable out there competing with other guys to become partner, chief surgeon, or chief executive officer. The testosterone coursing through our veins ensures this focus for most of us. This often means a man will spend long hours at the office as he works his way to the top. He will be preoccupied with work problems, issues or projects when he is at home or even out on a date. Most women just don't understand that a man who wants to "make it" in his profession has to give his job a major portion of his attention. This is a very important fact for women to realize—especially because a man's level of commitment to a relationship is directly related to his commitment to his career.

Even women with careers of their own often don't under-

stand the tremendous instinctual and cultural pressures a
man feels to succeed in the workplace. Many women head
down a dead-end street nagging, complaining, and pressuring their man to pay as much attention to their relationship as
he does to his career. They don't grasp that career advance-
ment is the one and only path most men can take to feel
proud and confident about themselves and what they are able
to provide for their girlfriends, fiancées, or wives. A woman
who supports her man and his ambitions is one who will be
greatly appreciated. You should learn this important truth
now. For if you do not understand or allow your man to act
upon his natural devotion to and passion for competing at
work, then your relationship with him will ultimately fail.

Don't try to tell us that a little ambition isn't attractive to
you women, either. We know how enticing the power and
money that come with a man's success can be. But time and
energy are the prices we pay to get to the top. Though sometimes we sacrifice everything to establish ourselves and get
ahead, usually we have some resources available to meet
women and build strong relationships with them as well.

We realize that women's careers are very important, too.
The aim of this book is to show women what they can do to
get a man to commit. We are presenting a one-sided view
that is simplified. We do support women's careers and hope
they succeed. But to get a man to commit, you must be sensitive to what work means to him and not compete with him.

The Career Game

From a very early age men are trained to be competitive,
whether we are playing a dodge ball game in grade school,
winning a high school football game, or rooting for our col-

lege basketball team. To be honest, this is superficial competition. Sports have very little to do with the outcome of the rest of our lives.

When it comes to our careers, a different style of competition exists. It's an internal type of competition. In order for a man to feel like a man, he has to be successful. As a professional, a man satisfies this need for competition and success by climbing the financial and career ladder. He needs to know that he can rise above the rest and become a good provider—not only for himself—but for his significant other and, eventually, for his children, too. It's not a sexist thing, don't get us wrong, it's just how it is. (Yes, we know that women work and provide as well—again, here we're just focusing on the male point of view.)

If a woman does not understand what stage a man is at in his career, it will be difficult for her to know what he needs from her and what he is able to contribute to a relationship. In such a situation, the relationship will quickly come to a dead end. These relationships are often characterized by a lack of understanding between a man and a woman. Stress, wasted time, and ultimately heartache are the outcome as a woman tries to make a man choose between her and the job.

The Three Career Stages

As you read in Chapter 2, we have observed that professional careers have three distinct stages. Since we happen to be in the medical, legal, and business professions, we tend to speak for men more like ourselves—men with typical, white-collar careers. This is not meant to demean men who are artists, athletes, blue-collar workers, and the like. In fact, we believe that all types of men will agree with most of what we have to say, especially men who are serious about excelling at what they do for a living (and what woman wants a man who isn't serious about working and prospering?).

Here we will describe the three career stages in greater detail and reveal what we are looking for in that special woman in our lives at each stage. Once a woman can identify what stage a man is at in his career, she will be able to know what he needs from her at each stage. Empowered with this knowledge, she will be able to make a decision as to whether or not she can give a man what he needs and whether she's ready to accept what he's willing to give her back. With our help, you will stop seeing his career as your competition, and you will learn how to complement a man on his way to the top. This approach will not only help you continue to bridge the communication gap between you and your man, but it will allow you to foster a better, longer-lasting relationship that will lead to the commitment finish line—getting married.

The Not-Yet-Set Stage

The first career stage a man enters is the Not-Yet-Set Stage. As you know in today's dog-eat-dog world, it's very difficult for a man to get established and settle into his career. A man doesn't necessarily have to be in the Not-Yet-Set Stage when he first begins working as a professional, and he can be in the Not-Yet-Set Stage fifteen years later.

Chris has experienced this in his career. When Chris first got out of college, he knew for sure that he wanted to be a partner in a public accounting firm. Embarking on his career, Chris basically bypassed the Not-Yet-Set Stage, because he was doing well and was being promoted in a timely fashion at his firm. He was well on his way to his goals.

As time progressed, Chris's career goals changed. The longer he worked in public accounting, the more he was exposed to the business world. He realized that there were more opportunities out there that he wanted to explore rather than graduating to partner in a Big Five accounting firm. After obtaining his M.B.A., he made a career move he viewed as a stepping-stone to what he ultimately wanted to do. After seven years as a certified public accountant, Chris made the move into the finance arena. He went from being strictly a C.P.A. to taking a larger role with broader business responsibilities as a controller for an Internet company. There he was, at twenty-eight years old, changing careers and entering the Not-Yet-Set Stage.

Rich, on the other hand, had planned to go to medical school since his eighth-grade science class. Once Rich got accepted to medical school, a definite career path was set. There were four years of medical school and six years of residency training for him. Preparing to become a practicing physician is a long, hard road, but one that is clearly mapped out. The only transitions are after medical school and after residency. During these transition periods, Rich had to choose his medical specialty.

Telltale Signs of the Not-Yet-Set Stage

The Not-Yet-Set Stage is characterized primarily by an unsure future. It usually entails some sort of new venture, whether it is a first job right out of school or a switch in industries, career paths, or job descriptions. A man is often uncertain about taking this new route as well as about succeeding in the new environment. At the Not-Yet-Set Stage a man will often discuss the validity of his newly made decision. (It's hard to make a decision and not look back.) He will commonly second-guess himself as he makes his way through this trial by fire. When a man is in this stage, he also works extra-long hours to learn his new craft and accomplishes an enormous amount of work in an effort to make a good impression. In the Not-Yet-Set Stage a man may even show signs of depression. It usually takes time to make a good impression at the office. Even when a man does make a good impression it sometimes goes unrecognized or unrewarded for a while. A man going through this challenging time in his career may experience unhappiness with his new work environment, doubt in his ability, a lack of trust in colleagues and coworkers he's competing against, concern about his future, and a longing to return to his previous career path.

Where Does Love Fit In?

This sounds challenging, doesn't it? You are probably thinking that a man at the Not-Yet-Set Stage of his career has no time, energy, or desire to become romantically involved with a woman. On the surface this seems to be the case, but we are here to give you the good news: it's not true. It is quite possible for a man who is in the Not-Yet-Set Stage to enjoy a committed, monogamous relationship that will eventually lead to engagement and marriage. As we always say, it is not so much a matter of timing as it is a matter of meeting the right woman. The right woman knows what to do to keep her man happy in a relationship—regardless of his career stage.

Many women have described to us the hardworking, highly driven professional men they used to date. From their descriptions, it was clear to us that these men fell into the Not-Yet-Set Stage, and these women blamed the relationship's failure on their feeling that, "He just wasn't ready." A statement like this is just more evidence to us that women simply don't understand men. We know just as many men who loved the women they were with while they were at this stage in their careers, but the lack of understanding and communication between the couple ultimately led to the relationship's downfall. At this stage, men are thinking that they must be on a strong career path if they are going to be able to provide for a woman and children down the road. A woman must understand that long hours at the office for him at this stage do not signify a rejection of her by the white-collar guy, but an investment he makes for their future together. We are not placing any blame on either party here. We are explaining what men are thinking at this stage and why many perfectly good relationships have crashed and burned.

Let's take a look at some friends of ours. Joe and Ashley are in a committed long-term relationship. Joe considers Ashley a woman with "wife potential." Joe is a lawyer who just started a job at a prestigious firm he has wanted to work for since graduating from law school. Everything seems new, and Joe is insecure. He is worried that his new boss won't see and acknowledge his talent and hard work. He fears that Tom, a coworker, will receive the promotion to the only higher position open in the firm. Joe works long hours and is often agitated by work-related concerns when he's with Ashley. In fact, if you asked him what the most stable thing in his life is—the thing he can count on most at this point— he would tell you it is his relationship with his girlfriend.

Since Joe is a man, and men are poor emotional communicators, Joe is not telling Ashley how he is feeling about his career—or their relationship. Since he started this new job, Ashley is not getting the warmth, emotion, love, and attention she is accustomed to receiving from Joe. She is feeling the burning need to "discuss the relationship" with Joe. (Does this scenario sound familiar to you?)

Ashley tries to discuss the relationship with Joe and what happens? Now Joe feels as if the only stable and enjoyable thing in his life and in his future has a "problem." Otherwise, why would his girlfriend want to have "a talk"? The last thing Joe wants to discuss or focus on is his relationship. He is preoccupied with his fledgling career and feels threatened by Ashley's request for a relationship status analysis. At this point, he is reluctant to level with her and to admit to her that he is scared and insecure about his career.

Ashley has now triggered a whole chain of revelations in Joe's mind. He suddenly perceives he is in a committed relationship. Sure, he knew about it before, but now it is front and center. Now all of Joe's fears have come into play. He starts wondering, Can I be a good provider for her? What if I fail, what will she think of me? What if I don't like what I'm doing and I need to start over, will she want to wait? Holy shit! I can't handle all of this pressure. On top of it, Ashley is the only woman I am ever going to sleep with for the rest of my life! *Oh no, I'm in a committed relationship, I'm done!* Now Joe will either back down and emotionally withdraw from Ashley, or he will take the extreme step of bailing out of the relationship altogether.

We're not placing blame on the women in strained or failed relationships. Mutual lack of understanding and communication are responsible for breakups at this stage. Now that you know what men are feeling in the Not-Yet-Set Stage, we will tell you what we need from you at this critical time in our careers.

What Women Can Do

First and foremost, you must recognize that men need *continuous votes of confidence and positive reinforcement.* It is very comforting for a man to know that the woman he loves has confidence in him, no matter what he does. Whether it is his first job out of college or a career change at thirty years old, it is extremely helpful for a man to have a woman about whom he cares in his corner, positively reinforcing that he is hardworking, has a lot to offer, and will be successful in anything he does. Think about it. When you are in a trying time in your life, isn't it helpful when the man you are dating is on your side telling you that you will succeed and that he is proud of you and has tremendous confidence in you?

Second, it is very helpful at this stage of a man's career if the woman he loves *takes an interest in his new venture.* It is music to a man's ears to hear his girlfriend ask how his day went, or inquire about his new coworker, or how an important meeting transpired. Show him that you are paying attention to what he tells you and that you want to do anything you can to help him face the challenges he inevitably will meet on his way to the top. This genuine interest makes a man feel as if he is not going through his new endeavor alone, which is exactly how many men feel as they struggle with new career challenges. A loving team member is a blessing in his situation; the moral support you can provide a man at this stage of his career path is invaluable.

Third, a woman should ensure that she and her man *do things together to help get his mind off his career.* As we mentioned, men feel an inordinate amount of pressure when they are in the Not-Yet-Set Stage of their careers. They have to learn a new industry or job, impress their colleagues and their superiors, and they always have to compete against others in similar roles. At this very stressful time, it would be immensely helpful to a man to get involved in activities that can help get his mind off his job, to remind him that he is in a wonderful caring relationship that allows him to spend quality "mindless" time with his girlfriend and just to blow off steam.

Your man probably won't have the time or energy to ensure that he has these stress-reducing opportunities on his calendar. This is where you can be helpful to him once again. You can be the equivalent of the cruise director for your man. Who better than you to plan fun activities for the guy you love? You know him better than anyone, and you know his schedule. So, focus on getting some fun into his life—and yours. Get the calendar out and plan:

- Weekend trips to ski, hike, or explore a nearby nature preserve
- A lunchtime visit to the park to read the newspaper and enjoy one another's company
- A Saturday movie festival where you vege out with popcorn in front of the VCR
- An afternoon at a nearby museum, theater, or ballpark
- A day shopping for things he likes—tools, clothes, music, or books
- A romantic evening at your favorite restaurant
- A picnic with friends you haven't seen in a while
- A workout schedule where you both meet at the gym

A few outings like these will take the worry lines out of your boyfriend's forehead and get him laughing again. Just see how much he appreciates you and enjoys himself once he stops thinking about job pressures for a few minutes. These activities will reduce his stress level and increase the chances of success at home, in his long-term relationship with you!

To Keep Him, Keep Calm

We have found that the Not-Yet-Set Stage is a difficult time for relationships. It can be very hard on a woman's patience, according to our female friends. They say that men are so focused on their new environments and trying to make strides to get to the next stage of their careers that they seem to forget that relationships need some of their time and energy. There's often no talk of moving in together, getting engaged, getting married, or having children. This often leaves a woman feeling insecure because it seems to her that the relationship is not a top priority for her man. This feeling leads many a woman to break off a relationship with a man who is at this stage of his career.

We're here to tell you that a relationship often is very important to a man at this stage. Most men depend strongly on their girlfriends during this time—you are the only stable thing in his life. Though a man may not talk about marriage or children, that doesn't mean they're not on his mind. To him, these things seem out of reach at this stage. In order for a man to be completely comfortable in a relationship and to begin to think about getting engaged, he must first know for sure that he has his feet on the ground financially. Try to understand what an important time this is in his career and avoid broaching such "relationship" topics as moving in together or getting engaged. Pushing a man toward commitment at this juncture is a recipe for disaster, because it embodies a man's greatest fear—being in a committed relationship without really knowing if he can be the provider he wants to be and feels he should be.

Rich has seen just how a woman's behavior at the Not-Yet-Set Stage helped his friend Phil pop the question to his girlfriend, Sue. Phil is in his residency and planning to be a neurologist, and Sue works as an office manager in a law firm. Sue had the faith and confidence to let Phil commit when he was ready, which happened to be two years and three months after they met.

Phil spent a long time looking for Sue, a beautiful woman who understands the demands of his medical career. Since he started dating her, Phil received from Sue nothing but support and understanding for his dream to become a neurologist. As their relationship became more serious, Phil didn't feel pressure from Sue about the time he spent working or the status of his feelings for her. Soon he was spending all of his free time with Sue. She became the best friend and confidante who made him feel at ease. Phil talked to Rich about how Sue was always there at the end of his long shifts, willing to lend an ear and share a smile with him. Although he kept it to himself, Phil was thinking what a great wife Sue would make. Two years of dating passed and Sue had not once pushed Phil to move in or get married. She was focused on her work at the office and knew she and Phil had a future together that would unfold when he felt comfortable to make a move. And it did, without one word of prodding from her. Three months later Phil asked Sue to be his wife and she happily accepted.

Like Sue, you can solidify your relationship with a Not-Yet-Set Stage man. In the first column are some comments you might feel like making but shouldn't. Look at the second column for the kind of reassuring statements your guy will appreciate:

Don't Say	Do Say
"You have no time for me."	"You are working so hard, what can I do to help you relax?"
"All you ever talk about is your job."	"Tell me what you did today. I'd love to hear what happened."
"Are you in love with your job or with me?"	"I know how important this [promotion, new job] is to you. Do what you have to and land it. I'll be here to celebrate when you get it."
"I had planned on getting married and having children before I turned fifty, which seems to be your time line."	"I love you and am glad that I can help you accomplish goals that will make a firm foundation for our future."

The Comeback/Starting-Over Stage

There is another stage related to the Not-Yet-Set Stage. This is the Comeback/Starting-Over Stage. This phase of a man's career is when he's proving himself again or starting to make a comeback. He may have recently changed his position or career, gotten fired or laid off, or is having a hard time finding a job.

Basically, a man going through this phase has it rough. Changing positions is very challenging and losing a job carries the same demands of a new job along with financial worries and psychological repercussions. Whereas a man who moves ahead to a higher position has new challenges and the pressure to perform them well, a man who is let go feels beaten but still has to find a new career track in which he can succeed. Getting fired or downsized is embarrassing. A man who has lost a job suffers a tremendous blow to his ego. He's probably asking himself, "How could this happen to me? Everything I've worked and hoped for is gone." You might find him withdrawn as he tries to work through the situation in his mind. A man who has chosen to take a new position or is looking for one can also be highly insecure about what other people think of him.

A man in the Comeback/Starting-Over Stage will forever remember a woman who supports him through the tough times. She is also probably the one person he will let help him get back on his feet. He will keep a brave face—not showing his humiliation—to most of the world. Be as supportive and understanding as you can if you are ever with a man who is in this vulnerable phase. Do all you can to bolster his ego, ease his stress, and help him take the practical steps he needs to get back into the game.

Ralph and Tracy are one couple that Chris knows whose relationship has flourished in spite of Ralph's experience with a tough Comeback/Starting-Over Stage. Tracy's loving support during a trying time for Ralph helped them become closer.

Ralph, a partner in his own law firm for ten years, and Tracy, who worked part time in a small retail clothing shop, had been living together for a year when Ralph was diagnosed with a heart condition. Hospitalized for two months, Ralph was forced to close his firm and let go of the big salary that went with it. When Ralph was leaving the hospital his doctor told him that the stress of running his own law office would hinder his recovery and advised Ralph to find a more flexible position that required fewer hours and less responsibility. Ralph did that, accepting a job as an associate at a small law firm nearby. This change made it difficult for him and

Tracy to pay the rent on their large Manhattan apartment. Tracy began working full time as a secretary and they both scaled back their expenses, adopting a modest lifestyle they could afford.

Through it all Tracy repeatedly assured Ralph that she loved him and not the money he had made. She said that her new job was exciting and rewarding and that she was happy to help out in any way she could. With her words and actions, Tracy made it clear to Ralph that she would stay with him even if he never regained his former salary level. Four months after he left the hospital, Ralph proposed to Tracy. He knew he had found the woman for him, the one who loved him and would stick by him no matter what.

If your man is going through a similarly tough time, you can follow Tracy's example with these words of support:

Don't Say	Do Say
"Loser, what happened to you? How are we going to survive?"	"We can make it through this together. What can I do to help?"
"I can't wait around any longer. My friends are getting married and having children already."	"What is important now is coming up with a new plan to deal with this situation. Let's talk about our options."
"My friend Marie's husband just got a big promotion at work yesterday."	"I know that once you set your sights on a goal you'll accomplish it. Don't worry about how long it takes, just give it your best shot. I'll be right here to support you."

What Women Can Do

- Listen. A man in this stage needs to express what's on his mind. You should listen to him as he sorts out his thoughts, feelings, and concerns. Don't pressure him to "unburden his soul" all the time, but when he does start to talk about what he's going through, listen. Show compassion by asking questions that will allow him to share his feelings without wounding his pride. Give him as much time as he needs to tell you about his disappointments, fears, regrets, and hopes. You are probably the only one he is sharing these things with.

- Give him positive reinforcement. Remind him of all of his great attributes. Help him to believe in himself as he works his way to the top or makes a comeback. Tell him you love him no matter what. Express your admiration for how he's coping with a period of extreme challenge or adversity.

- Be comforting; reassure him that this is another hurdle that he can conquer. Tell him that the two of you will get through this together. Offer encouragement whenever you can.

- Be patient. Give your man time and space to work through this period. Try not to take offense if he's withdrawing. Often men don't understand all they are feeling when they are in a flat-out sprint to get ahead or all of their future plans are blown out of the water by an unexpected turn of events. Sometimes they need time and space to think things through before they verbalize their feelings.

What Women Shouldn't Do

- Don't be another source of pressure. Whatever you do, don't bring up the relationship in a concerned tone to a man in the Not-Yet-Set or Comeback/Starting-Over Stage. He is not in the right frame of mind to talk about this. A man, absolutely, positively, won't respond as you'd like him to if you bring up the subject of marriage now. If you value your relationship at all, chill out and let the man set the pace.

• Don't be a sniper. If a man was recently shot down in his career, the last thing that he needs is to get shot down in his relationship, too. You should avoid introducing heavy topics that could potentially lead to a fight.

• Don't kick him while he's on the way up or down for the count. He's feeling insecure and sensitive; don't tease him about his low status on the career ladder or the fact that he was just sent to the bottom rung again. Don't point out tremendous strides being made by friends' or acquaintances' husbands. Focus on his strong points in conversations you have and comments you make. Do all you can to boost his self-confidence now.

• Don't talk endlessly about your job. Basically stay clear of job-focused conversations unless he starts them himself. Your accomplishments or trials will only start the endless parade of worries about his job performance or recent setback going again. Do what you can to keep conversations light and hopeful.

• Don't pity him. He will hate you for it.

• Don't be a fair-weather friend. In other words, if you're interested in a long-term relationship with this man, recognize that you have to be there for one another through life's trials

and unexpected downturns. Stick with him during this challenging time and show him that you are an ally he can trust no
matter what the situation. It will gain you big points when
your man is ready to move toward greater commitment.

If you stick it out and support your man through this
tough time, he will greatly appreciate your love, help, and
company. As he makes his way up to the top in his profession
or breaks through this current setback—be it big or small—
you'll both be there to benefit on the other side.

What Will You Get Out of It?

In this situation, the woman has the power to comfort and
invigorate a man. You can improve the relationship by making him feel better about himself. He'll always remember
that you were there for him through a trying time. He'll also
bond with you in a way that will make him more sensitive to
things you might be going through at work or in other family relationships down the road. In short, the two of you will
forge a deeper bond of communication and caring than
you've ever had before if you stand by your man now. In
addition, your man will recognize that you do have what it
takes to handle whatever life serves up. Men like this quality
in their wives. Need we say more?

The Transition Stage

So your boyfriend has chosen a career path, landed the job of
his dreams (or the job that could lead to the job of his
dreams), proved himself, performed well in his career, and is
now past the Not-Yet-Set Stage. We call this next stage the
Transition Stage. This is the point in a professional man's
career where he's defined his professional identity in a spe-

cific industry, and he's on a career path that makes him happy. He is good at what he does and has proven himself with his strong performance. Now he's ready to position himself to reach for the stars and become a great success.

Signs of the Transition Stage

The Transition Stage of a man's career is characterized by a marked increase in confidence and sense of direction. There's no clear-cut time frame when this stage occurs. Since all three of us have entered the Transition Stage, we will use our own careers to provide you with real-life examples of what to look for during this particular period.

The Transition Stage is heralded by a proven pattern of success. For example, before Chris reached the Transition Stage he had passed the C.P.A. exam, obtained his M.B.A. in finance, and had risen to the position of manager in a Big Five accounting firm. Before Brad entered the Transition Stage, he had passed the bar exam and completed a four-year tenure as a prosecutor in the district attorney's office, working on numerous cases and acquiring knowledge and experience within his profession. Rich entered the Transition Stage after completing medical school, enduring a grueling and challenging residency, becoming chief resident, and ultimately deciding where to practice medicine.

We are not giving you this list of accomplishments to blow our own horns. What we are trying to show you is how challenging and demanding a man's career is. A tremendous amount of time and effort is required to learn one's craft and to gain the experience and credibility needed for success.

The Transition Stage encompasses an intense time of change, as a man takes his career to the next level. In the

Transition Stage, a man has a lot more confidence. He feels that no matter what choices he makes he will always land on his feet. You might witness your boyfriend thinking about making a career move to the next level much as Brad did when he left the prosecutor's office to start his own firm, as Chris did by leaving public accounting to become a chief financial officer, and as Rich did by accepting the chief resident position at his hospital. Such decisions build up a man's career—and his confidence—to ultimately help him make his mark in his chosen branch of the professional world.

Beware of Transition Stage Show-offs

Sometimes men's Transition Stage career confidence spills over into their social lives—and gives them more confidence with women. Some men stupidly think that money brings power and that all they have to do is walk into a bar or night-club with their wallet pasted to their forehead and they will instantly attract a beautiful, intelligent woman. Women, beware of men parading their newly discovered earning power. This is not the type of man with whom you want to get involved if marriage is your goal.

Sam, an acquaintance of ours, started acting terribly when he hit the Transition Stage. As a C.P.A. who had landed a high-paying position with a venture capital firm, he soon became this flashy guy who was embarrassing to be around. He drove his new convertible Porsche to the Hamptons with his twenty-five-dollar cigars neatly tucked into his portable humidor. When he got to his beach house destination, he'd step out of the car wearing Gucci shoes and Armani sun-glasses, pausing dramatically before entering the party there. As transparent as this guy may seem, we have met many women who get caught up with men like this and inevitably are led astray and hurt.

Commitment Will Come

During the Transition Stage men begin to focus on relationship issues. Yes, it is true, men do think about these things and quite often do want to settle down, get engaged, get married, and start a family. The Transition Stage comes with a new sense of power, confidence, and achievement.

We each reached the Transition Stage at about the same time in our careers, approximately ten years after graduating from college. We had paid our dues by studying as undergraduates and then graduate students, and by learning and growing in our respective professions. Socially, we played the field pretty hard and met and dated many different women along the way.

The culmination of all of these years of hard work finally started to pay off. As our careers became more demanding, we naturally seemed to want to spend less time living the single life and partying so hard. Sure, we like to go out and let off some steam, but the week of five to seven late-night outings has become a distant memory.

During the Transition Stage both Brad and Rich committed to the women of their dreams, and all of the pieces to the puzzle fell into place. Keep in mind that these successful relationships were not about timing, but about meeting the right person who understood the stages that a man goes through as he heads toward commitment.

Rich is living proof of the fact that Ms. Right may turn up before a man is confident of himself in his profession or has reached many of his career goals. If a woman plays her cards right, she will head down the aisle with Mr. Right, no matter what stage of his career he happens to be in when they meet. Rich met Marla during his first year of residency training—while he was in the Not-Yet-Set Stage of his career. Rich recognized Marla as a potential wife right away. As long as he could pursue his career without any interference from his relationship, and as long as the relationship continued to progress, he was comfortable with Marla being the one for him even at such an early stage in his career.

They dated for three years before moving in together. At that time, Rich knew that Marla wanted to get engaged but toward the end of his residency he had to decide on his next career transition. He was now in the Transition Stage. As much as he loved her and wanted to marry her, he knew the time wasn't right for him with regard to his career. Once Rich accepted a post-residency position, he was then mentally ready for the whirlwind that comes with planning a wedding. Rich knew how important this time in his and Marla's life would be and wanted to wait for the perfect moment to begin their new life together. Only a few weeks after accepting his new position, Rich proposed to Marla. It had been six months since he and Marla moved in. They set the big date for a year later.

Marla also had incredible patience during Rich's Transition Stage. Rich admired and respected Marla because of her patience. In fact, it was one of the main reasons why he asked her to marry him. Marla understood what Rich was going through during his career Transition Stage. She did not constantly harp on engagement and marriage even though they had been dating for three years. Because of Rich's actions, Marla was confident that Rich was committed to her and would eventually propose.

The Right Woman

The woman to whom a man is likely to commit while in transition will probably be at a similar point in her life. She will be confident and secure in her future and will be comfortable thinking about moving a relationship to the next level of commitment. Not only should she be on the same page as her man is, but she should be just as independent.

Since *What Men Want* was published, we have constantly been asked how men feel about women who have successful careers or about women who make more money than we do. Do we feel threatened? Are we jealous? Is it a turnoff? Well, quite honestly, we find it very attractive. We love it when a woman is confident and independent and has a career. We think it's incredibly important for a woman to have a fulfilling life of her own.

A man in the Transition Stage would rather not talk much about his professional life when he comes home. Sure it is fine to let a girlfriend know what is going on at the job, but at this stage, there's so much pressure and so much hard work that when we get home, the last thing we want to do is talk about it. What do we want to talk about? Our girlfriends' active, engaging, fulfilling lives, that's what. It is exciting to hear about something new and different from our careers. Focusing on his girlfriend's activities also helps a man get his mind off his stressful work environment.

Rich found that this certainly was the case for him. As a physician, every day is stressful for Rich. He has to make critical decisions in the office and in the operating room about his patients' health and lives. The last thing he wants to do is to bring these stresses into his personal life. In fact, Rich makes a point of not discussing his stressful days with his fiancée, Marla. He discusses an exciting surgical procedure or an interesting case with her now and then, but he does not want to rehash his worries every single day at home. Instead, Rich likes to hear about Marla's day at work as an international tax planner. He's interested in her career and listening to her helps him relax after a busy day. He finds it quite fascinating to hear Marla talk about life in corporate America and the projects on which she works. Aside from working full time, Marla is also pursuing her M.B.A. at Villanova. Rich enjoys helping her with her business school studies when she asks for his assistance. He values the fact that he and his wife-to-be have entirely different careers from one another and finds it extremely refreshing to talk about something other than medicine at the end of his day.

Of course, there are some days when Rich does not want to talk to anyone when he gets home. On these incredibly stressful days, he comes home, quickly eats dinner, and goes straight to bed. Marla understands this and gives Rich space when he needs it. Rich does the same for her. This understanding has helped their relationship tremendously.

When Brad comes home from work, the last thing he wants to do is revisit all that went on that day. Brad is extremely busy at work and enjoys hearing what his wife Cheryl did during her workday. Cheryl works in a large department store as a personal shopper handling the individual shopping needs of celebrities and affluent individuals. She is extremely talented in her ability to relate to her diverse list of customers. To Brad, it seems as though Cheryl always comes home with a good story about one of her celebrity clients. He enjoys hearing what goes on in her day and also finds it very challenging to try to assist Cheryl in increasing her sales productivity. Brad enjoys seeing Cheryl's success when he watches, say, an awards show—and sees a celebrity outfitted by his wife.

What you say to a man in the Transition Stage can hurt—or strengthen—the relationship. Here's a list of what not to say contrasted with a list of what to say to a man in the Transition Stage (Cheryl and Marla actually made the positive comments in the Do Say column to Brad and Rich):

Don't Say	Do Say
"Are we ever going to get married? Do you think about it at all—Or am I waiting around for nothing?"	"Let me tell you a funny thing that happened at work today."
"Let me get this straight, I'm not going to see you at all this week? Why don't you e-mail me a photo so I can remember what the guy I'm supposedly seeing looks like."	"I will miss not seeing you this week, but I know how hectic your schedule is. Mine's the same. Don't blame me if I ravish you next Friday, though. I'm craving you something terrible!"
"Hello. Hello! It's nice to see you, too! I can't believe you were going to walk in the door and not even say anything to me!"	"I can see you are tired, honey. I left a snack and the paper there on the table. I know you want some peace and quiet. I'll be reading in bed if you need me."

What a Woman Can Do

• Concentrate on your own career or interests. A man in the Transition Stage of his career will look for a woman who can share her accomplishments and the activities of her day with him. He also looks for distraction from the stresses of his work in her conversation. Give him a chance to focus on what you are doing.

• Be patient. Many times men in the Transition Stage would love to move in or get engaged to their serious girlfriends, but they are still too focused on their careers to do so comfortably. They are looking ahead to a time of stability when they can provide for their women in the way they feel is right. Understand this and don't push.

- Give your man space. A man in the Transition Stage of his career is in the midst of a very challenging time at work. He will appreciate a woman who grasps this, giving him the alone time and space he needs after work or on the weekends to decompress.

The Successful Stage

Although some people would look at us and say that we are successful professionals, we feel that we are still in the Transition Stage of our careers and that we have a long way to go to reach our ultimate career goals and be considered "successful." So, we ventured out and spoke to our male family, friends, colleagues, and business associates who we felt were "successful" and asked their opinions about what success meant to them in terms of their careers and how this affected their relationships with women. We focused on single men or men who became single again during the Successful Stage of their careers.

The most important thing we were told by successful single men was that in order to be completely fulfilled they needed a woman whom they loved and who would love them back. Though they had already achieved success in their careers, they felt unfulfilled because they didn't have that special someone with whom to share their lives. They were financially stable and looked upon with a tremendous amount of respect and admiration. They had acquired a great deal of experience and were confident about their abilities. They had arrived. They had established a great track record and they knew that they could be successful in almost anything they wanted to do involving their careers.

So what were their biggest fears? We found that single men in the Successful Stage feared living alone. They wondered why they hadn't met that special someone—or why their earlier relationship hadn't worked out—and wondered if they ever would meet someone to whom they could permanently commit. They were concerned that women would "fall in love" with them because of what their position was instead of who they were. Though these guys were on top when it came to their careers, they all felt that something was missing in their lives without a special woman.

The successful men we spoke with were in search of a woman whom they could love and who would also be able to stand by their sides at any social or business functions. One of the men we spoke to summed it up perfectly when he said, "I want a woman I can talk to, a soul mate—someone I am comfortable with alone for a weekend after we've spent every weeknight going to social or business outings. I would be at ease with her out in front of a crowd or alone at home." Honesty and confidence in herself were the two qualities these successful men valued most highly in the woman with "wife potential."

So what can a woman do to help foster a relationship with a man who is at the Successful Stage of his career? Judging from what men at this stage told us, her true focus on the man for himself is of the utmost importance. Men were quite weary of "gold diggers." Any reference to his power or his fortunes was usually enough to make a man leave a woman behind and not look back.

On the other hand, these men were much more amenable to relationship talk and to discussing some deeper issues very early on than those of us who had not reached the Successful Stage. Honesty is the best policy in these conversations. Discussions about being married in the past or talks about the children a woman may have had from a prior marriage were all very important to these men. Successful men are sincerely interested in the way a woman sees her past experiences and future goals.

If you are dating a successful man, take a look at how you can get his attention with straightforward talk about yourself and thoughtful questions about him:

Don't Say	**Do Say**
"All you need to know about my ex is that he is a no-good SOB."	"My ex and I fell in love and got married, but we never communicated well. After a few years we seemed to lose the friendship we had."
"You've got the taste and money I like, you're not like the last guy I dated who thought a burger and a Coke in the car was a date."	" I enjoy our conversations. Your laughter and openness make me feel at ease."
"What do you do that brings in the kind of money that can pay for a Jaguar like this?"	"I am looking for a serious relationship with the right man, a man who would love me and my sons and be a good father to them."
"You are president, after all, you should have access to a ski lodge and Caribbean condo."	"I know you work hard, but what do you like to do when you are not working? What relaxes you and brings out that beautiful smile of yours?"

What a Woman Can Do

How can a woman attract the attention of a man in the Successful Stage of his career? Here are a few steps you can take to better your chances of moving a successful Mr. Right toward commitment.

•   A strong, confident approach works best—a nice smile, a firm handshake, and a happy disposition will start things off right.

•   Discussions about current events, sports, or family are great ways to make small talk. These topics are focused on things other than careers and money—and men in the Success Stage of their careers would much rather talk about these things than about their careers and what they do for a living every day. Remember, successful men are a bit paranoid that women are interested only in their money.

•   Surprising as it may seem from what we have told you about guys in general, men in the Successful Stage are much more interested in hearing about a woman's past relationships. They want to know what they are dealing with up front and don't want any surprises. Though you should feel free to talk about your past relationships with guys like these, be careful not to demonize your ex-husbands. If you do, the man you are talking to will think he could be the next addition to the list.

•   Take any opportunity offered to show him that you can be comfortable and stand on your own in any social setting. If you are a good conversationalist, hostess, and diplomat let him see that. Men at the Successful Stage often have a public life, so they need a partner who's socially adept. If you have attributes that help you in this arena be sure to let them shine.

- Be honest about what you are currently looking for in a man. This will put Mr. Successful at ease if he is interested in you, and it will also help you find out sooner rather than later if he could be your Mr. Right.

Why Is His Career So Important Anyway?

It is important to a man that his family, friends, bosses, and ultimately his girlfriend, all think that he is a hardworking and successful man. To be at peace with himself, a man must keep his career moving forward on a steady track. His competitive attitude toward his career has replaced his athletic and academic successes of high school and college.

Obviously, a man reaps other benefits with success as well—pride in his title, a good salary, hard-earned promotions or bonuses, and positive feedback from clients, peers, and bosses. Again, these things all stroke a man's fragile ego. Our society also places a lot of weight on a man to climb the corporate ladder. When things are going well in his career, a man feels as though he can relax a bit. He can ease back and bask in the tremendous amount of positive reinforcement he receives for performing as he should. He can be confident in himself and his accomplishments. This is why a man in the Successful Stage feels comfortable opening himself up more than most men in a relationship with a woman. From our experience, we know that a man must feel relatively at ease wherever he is in his career in order to have a successful serious relationship.

Chris can remember being promoted at a very quick pace at his first accounting firm. He wasn't quite satisfied, because he wasn't at one of the Big Five firms. He thought he could do better and really wanted to be with a larger, more competitive firm, where the big titles and promotions were. Chris was not ready to commit to a woman. To us, this was not a coincidence. We are not saying that if Ms. Right had happened to waltz into Chris's life at this juncture he would not have dated her with thoughts of a serious commitment down the line. What we are saying is that the point Chris was at on his career path would impact the way he approached commitment. This is the way it is for almost every professional man.

Once a man is in the working world, he begins to realize how difficult it is to make ends meet. He starts to see that the professional world is very competitive and starts to live by the saying "If you take lunch you are lunch." Whether this credo is true or just perceived, a man often applies a work philosophy that allows little time for play. He is fully dedicated and puts everything he has into being successful. Any naive dreams he had of being a professional baseball player or the leading man in blockbuster movies have faded away and reality has set in. A man with professional career goals soon sees that it's going to be a long road to success. He doesn't mind the challenge and the hard work, but he's realistic about just how much time, effort, and focus it is going to take to accomplish his goals.

This is when things become quite difficult for us as men. We do want to be successful in our careers, and we do want a loving, caring relationship with a great woman. The more committed we become to a woman, the more committed we become to our careers. We do struggle to find a balance. We have made many women very angry by missing dinners, working too late, and just not spending enough time together. It seems like a never-ending cycle to us. We work so hard to ensure success and financial comfort for ourselves and the women in our lives, yet sometimes we work so many hours that there's no time to build and enjoy a relationship. A man begins to feel as if he is married to his job. He starts to think, I better go into the office and go the extra mile because nobody reaches the top without hard work. If I'm not going to put in the effort, my company will suffer, and I know that there's someone else out there who is hustling and will soon eat me for lunch. A man wants to provide for himself and the woman in his life. He trains himself to be disciplined and to work hard, very hard, for financial comfort and success.

What Not *to Do*

We find it extremely frustrating when our girlfriends don't understand the pressures we have at work and, in their ignorance, add to them. Few things are as annoying as trying to finish up a demanding task or two at work while being interrupted every five minutes with a call from a girlfriend who is wondering what we are doing, why we haven't left yet, and when we will be home.

It is difficult enough for a man to be in the office late at night or on the weekends trying to get work done instead of enjoying a sunny day or a relaxing evening with the woman he loves. When this time stretches out because nagging calls break his thought process, a man could get very upset, angry, and resentful. Not only is the nagging irritating, but it brings on guilt. The hardworking man thinks, "I *should* be with her and not in the office. Why can't I ever seem to get done what I have to do and still have time to be with her?" Finally, all of this builds into a great ball of stress, leading him (if he's like most men) to blow his cool and lash out at his girlfriend, which always ends in a fight. Then he has to leave the office at 11 P.M. and search around town, trying to find some flowers, because he knows even though he's only trying to please this woman, he has yelled and now must make up with her, again.

We have witnessed this scenario unfold time and again with a close friend of ours. He is a very hardworking entrepreneur who is struggling to get his own business off the ground. He is in a long-term, committed, monogamous relationship with a woman whom he might have married by now. But she has shown her lack of understanding by constantly calling him at work and giving him a hard time about what he is doing, why he is working so hard, and when he will come home. Our friend just can't understand how the woman he loves can be so unsupportive. As painful as it has been for him, our friend has really begun to rethink whether this girlfriend is the Ms. Right he thought she was. Her nagging behavior about his work is the main reason he hasn't asked her to marry him. He probably never will.

We hate to miss a meal that the woman in our lives has prepared for us because we have to work late. Think about it—who wouldn't rather be sitting across from a lovely woman, eating dinner by candlelight, sharing a little wine, instead of troubleshooting a problem that arose late in the day at work? We are disappointed when we can't get away from the office at the time we said we would or, worse, must be late for a dinner that we have looked forward to all day. We know that our girlfriends are disappointed when this happens, but we hope they understand our situation. We don't appreciate the calls asking when we will be home. We want to be the ones to make the first call informing them we will be late and the second call to tell them we are on our way. In between these calls we want to be able to focus on the job at hand.

When we tell them we are running late, the women with

wife potential say, "Honey, don't worry. I know you are working hard and we will enjoy the meal when you are relaxed and finished with work. Take your time. Just give a call when you are ready to leave and I will reheat dinner so it will be warm when you arrive." If you want to keep your relationship moving toward commitment, you'll answer the same way. You may even want to further ease the pressure your man feels by saying, "Why don't we plan on a nice dinner out on Saturday so you don't have to worry about when you get home tonight. I'm going to go ahead and eat and will reheat your meal when you come home."

Positive Results

You may begin to notice that your relationship is at its best when work is going well for your boyfriend. He is probably very happy, extremely confident, and very energetic when he sees you, if all is going well on his career path. He relaxes and opens up a bit, his conversation with you improves, you seem to interact more smoothly, and soon you find you are sharing your lives and love in a relationship that has long-term potential. The sense of accomplishment he has when things go well at work makes a man feel proud, and he wants you to see him in this new light. He feels like the king of the mountain who is ready to take on anything. When he feels on-track with his career, your boyfriend might even feel more loving toward you. This is because a man often sees his success as something of real substance he can share with someone he loves.

You can win big points by sticking with a guy while he works his way up to where he wants to be. A man feels most secure with a woman when he sees that she can stand by him even during his most trying times. A man takes a woman's tolerance and understanding of his long hours, short temper, and bad moods during bumps on his road to success as great signs of love and affection. Though a man may not always be able to show or tell a woman that he appreciates her during the hard times, this is when he does need her patience, support, and love the most. There is a bigger payoff than appreciation. From what we've seen, relationships that have weathered the adversity that comes naturally with a man's rise to the top seem to lead to marriage. Do what you can to understand the trials your man faces in his career and help him through them.

We know a number of women who have bailed out on their boyfriends when these men were facing the biggest challenges in their careers. The men left behind lost their key source of emotional support just when they needed it most. Can you think of a worse situation? The men who've gone through this don't forget it. The woman who leaves doesn't either. She usually ends up regretting her choices and actions, wondering later as her ambitious ex becomes a success, "How in the world did I let that guy get away?"

We looked on with sympathy when this happened to Mike, a fellow C.P.A. Chris sat down the hall from and befriended during his time at the Big Five accounting firm. Mike had been dating Cindy, a petite architect with a funky style all her own, for a year. There was an instant attraction when they met at a downtown bar and they had gone on to build what seemed like a strong relationship, sharing their love of art, hiking, and old movies. Cindy's mother loved Mike and Mike's parents were delighted when their son brought Cindy home for Thanksgiving. She was just the kind of fun-filled, caring woman they hoped Mike would find. It seemed everyone was thinking this relationship had the long-term potential that Mike talked to Chris about.

Mike was considering taking the relationship to the next level when he was deluged with a series of unexpected crises. Within a two-month period, the boss who hired and liked Mike was replaced by a micromanaging power monger, Mike's rent was raised out of his price range, and a client he had done some accounting consulting for was audited and threatened to sue Mike as a result. Suddenly, Mike was looking for a new job, a new apartment, and a good lawyer. He had almost no time to spend with Cindy, and when they did get together he was distracted. They even stopped having sex. Mike was a wreck and Cindy didn't know how to handle the situation. She was hurt and angry that Mike wasn't calling as much, and he stopped inviting her out for those long dinners and late-night movies she loved. She almost never saw Mike anymore and he was a bundle of nerves when she did. Within a month, Cindy got fed up and broke it off with Mike. She told him he was a nice guy but that the relationship had become more work than fun and she just wasn't ready for that right now. Mike was heartbroken and felt as though the last leg of stability had been kicked out from under him. He implored Cindy to stick around—he was sure things would get better. She wouldn't.

Mike did pull through and now, five years later, runs his own very successful accounting firm. He has been dating but hasn't yet found anyone he connects with as much as he did with Cindy. It's too bad she couldn't have had a little more patience and understanding. If she had, then there would have been many rewards to reap, including the love of a resilient and successful man.

Here are some of the do's and don'ts you can follow to help your boyfriend ease into a committed relationship no matter what is happening on his career path:

• Always be supportive of your man's career and be prepared at times to take a backseat to it.

• Understand the three different career stages and know what career stage your man is in. Realize how each stage defines what your man can give to your relationship when he's making his way toward his career goals. Tailor your expectations of him and the relationship with these in mind.

• Provide a man in the Not-Yet-Set Stage of his career with votes of confidence and positive reinforcement. He appreciates a woman who takes an interest in his new venture, helps him get his mind off his career at times, and is willing to allow their relationship to evolve slowly as he focuses most of his attention on his work.

• Focus on your own life and goals when you are involved with men in the Transition Stage of their careers. Be patient when it comes to commitment. These guys need women who are independent and have lives of their own. Men greatly appreciate girlfriends who are confident and smart enough to help them reach important career goals that will set them well on their way to success.

• Show your experience, worldly wisdom, and honesty to a man in the Successful Stage. These guys need openness from a woman right from the start and like to move things along a little bit more quickly in a relationship. They want a woman to love them for who they are—not what they have or have accomplished.

• Stick around through the tough times and rewards will come.

Now you know the different career stages through which a man goes and his feelings toward commitment in each. This is very important knowledge to have when you are looking for the man with whom you hope to spend the rest of your life, since you want to optimize your chances at a successful relationship with him. Unless you are already seriously dating a professional man who you believe has you in his "wife potential" category, you will most likely meet your Mr. Right on the dating scene. In the next two chapters, we will cover how to spot a man who will commit and some of the steps you can take as you move through the early stages of dating to keep him in your life.

4
—

TROUBLESHOOTING COMMITMENT OBSTACLES: PART I

Blind Dating, On-line Dating, Dating Players, Fast-Start Relationships, and Dating at Work

When women have problems with a man's committing, it is usually for one of two reasons: either they fall in love with the wrong man or they mess things up with the right man. We want to help women avoid these two situations, so we thought long and hard about why they happen. The answer is simple (to us at least). We've found that women don't know when they are wasting their time with a guy who will never commit to them, or they try to force the right guy to commit before he is ready. The first scenario is what we will focus on in the next two chapters. In later chapters we will introduce you to the way men think about commitment to monogamy and engagement—and how to ease your man into both.

Weed Out Mr. Wrong or Better Your Odds with Mr. Right

Helene, a friend of Brad, liked to move relationships with men onto the fast track. She wasn't happy unless the relationship got serious quickly. "I'm almost thirty and don't have any time to waste," is how she justified her speedy jump into relationships time and again. Brad suggested to Helene that she should slow down when it came to men. He didn't like to see this friend he had known for years get hurt when smooth talkers and fast movers took advantage of her impatience. For years, Helene would tell Brad stories of passionate weekends with wildly attractive men who had lots of money and lots of style. But these stories always had the same ending—within two weeks, the calls had dropped off and Helene was nursing a broken heart. Brad told Helene these guys were just out for sex and were thrilled to find it with a beautiful woman like her, but that they were not going to commit to her. He gently told Helene that they were treating her like a "good for now" girl rather than a "marriage material" girl.

Then, Helene told Brad about Stan, a guy she had met on a blind date. He was a friend of Helene's roommate, Maggie. Helene said that she had been dating Stan in between her weekends with the guys Brad knew were players, and she thought she might be falling for him. Stan seemed sweet and considerate and, from what she told us, was interested in her for more than sex. Stan had just taken Helene on a romantic weekend upstate, the first night they had spent together since they started dating six months earlier. During the following week, Stan had called Helene several times to schedule a Saturday night date for the upcoming weekend and tell her how much he enjoyed their time in the cabin at Lake

George. It seemed to us like Helene was not the only one smitten.

Sure enough, Helene and Stan soon saw more and more of one another. Six months later they were dating each other exclusively. When Helene talked about Stan, she had wonderful things to say about his intelligence, humor, and good looks. But she always complained about his dedication to his family's import/export business. She said she felt as though she was competing with his work for time. Brad told her to be glad that she was dating someone with ambition. But Helene was impatient. When she and Stan had been dating eighteen months, she said she was going to "have a talk" with her boyfriend about her place in his life and how it seemed that his work took priority over her. Brad got very firm and serious with Helene when he heard this. He warned her that instead of trying to get Stan to spend less time on the business, she should spend more time talking to him about it. He told Helene to try showing a sincere interest in what Stan was doing business-wise and get back to him in a month.

Helene followed Brad's advice and she was excited to give him the update when she called. She said that it seemed as though Stan had been waiting for her to ask about the family business and was eager to talk about it. He started confiding in her about his worries and his plans. Much to her surprise, Helene said she actually became very engaged in what Stan was doing in import/export. Stan began bringing Helene to business and family functions he had only talked to her about before. From what Helene told Brad, this guy was getting closer to her and was probably thinking seriously of commitment. It was true. Helene called Brad four months later to tell him the happy news of her engagement and to thank him for his insight and advice.

*   *   *

There are red flags that indicate commitment obstacles to which we pay attention when we are dating. When these flags are flying during a date or a relationship, the women we are with aren't "marriage material" and will never walk down the aisle toward us wearing that white dress. Sometimes, we continue to date these "good for now" girls for sex, company, or just variety, as you know from *What Men Want*. This is exactly what you don't want to happen when you are looking to settle down with Mr. Right. Women like Helene are often blind to these hazards and stay in relationships that are going nowhere fast. As you saw in her case, we can help!

Sometimes, how you and the man you are dating respond to red flags can make all the difference in whether or not your relationship moves to the final round of commitment. We'll reveal how you can survive any danger zones you encounter. With a little help from us, you will be able to recognize situations, issues, and behaviors that indicate you are dating Mr. Wrong or are well on your way with Mr. Right.

Blind Dating

In general, we have found blind dating a very helpful system for meeting single, available women. The key to blind dating is the person doing the setting up. If the person who is arranging the date is a very good friend of yours, you can usually feel quite confident that the man you're meeting will have some of the qualities you find appealing. If the person setting you up is closer to your date than he or she is to you, the odds that you'll meet someone who'll match your expectations are considerably lower. You could be having drinks or dinner with Frankenstein, Kevin Costner, or anyone in between.

In the days when Brad was single, he had a close female friend who would set him up on blind dates. We'll call her Sandra. Brad always knew a blind date set up by Sandra was a safe bet. That's because Sandra knew him well, understood what he liked, and knew what he needed. Brad actually dated quite a number of women who met his criteria for looks, personality, and values through Sandra.

Lori was another woman who was a great resource for Brad during his dating years. Out one night at a bar, Brad met Lori and they had a great time talking. Lori was seeing someone but was very friendly and had a lot of single women friends. She liked spending time with Brad and thought maybe someone in her crowd would hit it off with him. She asked Brad if he would like to join her and a group of college friends the next night. Brad did and ended up going on a date with Amanda, one of Lori's college roommates. The relationship did not go farther than that, however, and when Brad told Lori what happened she invited him to go out again, this time with some women she knew from work. He agreed and ended up dating one of them for quite some time.

When you are dating, the key is to keep your eyes open and cultivate opportunities not only to meet people you are attracted to but to meet people who could introduce you to that special person as Brad did with Sandra and Lori.

Chris, on the other hand, is usually set up on blind dates by women who know him only through work, the gym, or a mutual friend. Their main interest is finding a date for their close female friends. Unfortunately, these acquaintances don't know Chris very well and, as a result, don't know what he likes in a woman. Most of the blind dates Chris has been on have not led to subsequent dates or long-term relationships.

The Approach

Blind dating can be an exciting way to meet new people, or it can be a humbling experience. It depends on how you approach each date. Before they were in committed relationships, Brad and Rich used to love going on blind dates. Every blind date was a new opportunity to meet an attractive woman, someone you might hit it off with, whom you otherwise would not have met. Brad and Rich admit that when they were being set up on blind dates, all they could think about was how hot the woman was going to be. This might sound superficial, but you can see the excitement with which these two looked forward to evenings with women they had never met before.

Chris's approach to blind dating is different. Rather than focusing on how impressed he'll be by his date, he is more concerned with how well the woman will receive him. If a woman he's met on a blind date doesn't want to see him again, Chris has a tendency to take this very personally. On the other hand, if Brad or Rich went on a blind date and it didn't work out, they would just chalk it up to incompatibility.

All three of us agree that a major advantage to blind dating is knowing that the woman whom we are taking out is willing and able to date. We assume this is so since the woman has given the go-ahead to be set up and provided her number for one of us to call her. In addition, a man set up on a blind date knows that his date is going to be expecting and even looking forward to his call. This removes a lot of the anxiety and insecurity a man feels about approaching a woman. When a man meets a woman on his own and gets her phone number, hanging over him always is the fear that he'll be blown off by her. We can't even count the times when we've called the number a woman has given us only to be asked what kind of pie we'd like by the local pizza place, or we have obediently left a message after the beep that would never be returned. With a blind date, at least a man's assured that the woman will be receptive to his initial attempts to get together. We all agree that this makes arranging the first date that much easier for us.

Ditch the Blind Date Stigma

Don't get depressed about blind dating. Many women are embarrassed that they can't find a man on their own and have to rely on friends to help them meet someone. Don't let this get you down. The reality is that dating has become much more difficult than it used to be.

Professionals in their late twenties or early thirties are much more mobile now than they were in the past. Many of us find ourselves in a new city, town, or state with few friends or acquaintances, never mind dates. Even if we aren't transferred, our careers seem to come first and working eighty hours a week has become the rule, not the exception. It is very difficult to meet people under these circumstances, so don't feel bad if you are blind dating. You never know, you just might meet a really attractive guy with a great personality who is as busy as you are and sees "wife potential" in you down the line. We can guarantee that if you saw that same guy on the train or at the Laundromat or in a bar, you would never have approached him.

Blind dating can also be an excellent remedy for those who are tired of the bar and night club scene. If you are not meeting Mr. Right on your own, there is nothing wrong with getting a little help from some friends. Being set up can be an excellent alternative to spending one of the few free nights you have out at a loud club where you meet no one and come home with your ears ringing. Just make sure it's a close friend who's doing the setting up—a person who knows what you are looking for in a guy will have the best chance of finding your Mr. Right.

As uncomfortable as blind dating is and as much as it seems like the odds are against you, remember that each blind date is completely independent of another. Each blind date brings a new chance to find love. There are plenty of happy marriages that began with a blind date. So let your friends know you're open to the idea. Look at blind dating as an opportunity and, hey, if you don't click with a guy you meet on one night out then you just aren't right for each other. Don't let a date with someone rude, unappealing, or just not your type stop you from going on blind dates for fear that the next one will be the same. Chances are that if the right person is setting you up things might just work out.

The Male Matchmaker

If you are looking for commitment with Mr. Right, you should be very wary about being set up on a blind date with a guy by one of his pals. Guys who are going through droughts will look to every resource they can in order to have sex. Sometimes the desire for sex forces a man to swallow his pride and ask his friends if they know anyone they can set him up with. Guys are quite accommodating because they grow tired of hearing their friends complain about their lack of action. If a guy gets set up on a blind date by a friend of his, it is usually just to help him get some sex.

Let's face it. Guys just aren't that deep when it comes to matchmaking. What guy knows a woman he's not dating well enough to make the determination that she will be good for his friend? There are exceptions, but in general, a guy who sets his friend up on a blind date with you is not thinking of your best interests. He is looking to jump-start his friend's sex life. If a relationship develops out of it that's great, but it's not the goal.

Here's another truth you might find surprising. The minute a male friend tells a guy that he has a woman for him to meet, he immediately thinks she must be second rate. If she's so great, then why wouldn't his friend be putting the moves on her? Guys aren't that generous. In fact, they are extremely territorial when it comes to outstanding women. Believe us, a man's first thought is not to set his friends up with great women. A man's first, second, and third thought is how he might be able to win her for himself.

The Female Matchmaker

You have a much better chance of finding a guy with long-term dating potential when women do the matchmaking. Women would rather see their guy friends and their girl-friends in caring, healthy relationships that extend far beyond one night of hot sex. So, naturally, a date that a female friend sets up for you has a greater chance for success when it comes to your intentions—meeting Mr. Right. We'd suggest you follow up on any such offers.

Remember Brad's friend Sandra? Sandra turned out to be such a great resource for Brad that Brad used to ask Sandra to go out to happy hours or go shopping just to be on the lookout for a girl to introduce to him. Brad was lucky to have such a great woman friend who was also a superb matchmaker. In fact, it was through a blind date set up by Sandra that Brad eventually met his wife, Cheryl. A friend like Sandra could very well introduce you to Mr. Right.

Inside Your Blind Date's Mind

Though the pressure of the call to arrange a meeting with a woman is lessened for us with a blind date, planning the date comes with its own set of challenges and questions. Do I take her to dinner? No, too formal for a blind date. Drinks? Well maybe she doesn't drink and, after all, it is a weeknight. Go for a cup of coffee? Well, if we do that and it works out and I want to kiss her good night, I'm going to have coffee breath. Is she going to like me? Maybe I'm too short or too tall or maybe I'm not good enough for her. What if I don't like her? How will I let her down easily? What will I tell the person who tried to make a match? These are all very common things that go through a man's mind before he goes on a blind date.

When it comes to the date itself, men always arrange a quick-out option in case the girl he meets turns out to look like the Bride of Frankenstein. On the flip side, if the woman who opens the door resembles Cindy Crawford, he is clever enough to suddenly have nowhere to go until work the next morning. On a blind date, looks are extremely important. (Don't tell us you don't feel the same way!) Since we don't know a blind date, how she appears when we first meet is all we have to go on. We like to see a woman who has put on her best face (without overdoing the makeup) and is well groomed, dressed nicely without looking like a fashion victim. We always want to make a good first impression on a woman, so you can be sure most guys will turn up showered, shaved, and appropriately dressed.

Blind Dates We Have Heard About and Been On

Nice, But No Spark

A few summers ago, Chris's friend Tony was set up by an acquaintance he met in a beach house. Although this match-maker didn't know Tony very well, she tried to set him up with a very close friend of hers, Meryl. She described Meryl to Tony in a way that led him to believe that they were perfect for each other. When Tony finally met Meryl, she couldn't have been farther from his type. The two of them still had an enjoyable evening together. Throughout dinner, they found that their personalities did seem to match somewhat, and they did get along quite well. But this did not change the fact that Tony was not very attracted to Meryl. Even though they had an enjoyable evening, they never went out again.

Many blind dates can be fun and still not result in another meeting. Make the most of each one you have and keep an optimistic outlook.

Too Late, Too Tall: No Match

A friend of ours, Alex, was set up on a blind date by a woman he knew from the office. The matchmaker didn't know either Alex or Anne, the woman with whom she was setting him up, very well. She built Anne up to be the girl of Alex's dreams and gave him her number. Alex called. After he and Anne spoke a few times on the phone, they made a date.

When Alex arrived at Anne's apartment building, he told the doorman whom he was there to see. Anne told the doorman she would be right down. So Alex waited . . . and waited . . . and waited; he waited for what seemed to be an eternity. (Men hate the insincere "I'll be right down" line. It makes them feel incredibly uncomfortable.) As the moments slipped by, Alex became increasingly self-conscious. He was convinced that the doorman was looking at him funny—as if he knew he was there for a blind date. Every time the elevator bell chimed, Alex sat up and looked as the doors opened, smiling at every woman as she stepped off the elevator, thinking that this was Anne, at last. Needless to say, he got a few strange looks. Finally, Anne did get off the elevator. She was quite attractive and had a very nice body. Unfortunately, Anne was much taller than Alex was. This was something she didn't like—and neither did he. They went out for a few beers, but they both knew that it would be an early night, and they wouldn't be seeing each other again. This was very uncomfortable for Alex. In the future he would think twice before agreeing to be set up by someone who didn't know him well.

Let this be a lesson about matchmakers—stick with good friends. Also, if you want to make a good first impression, don't keep your date waiting.

It's Not Over Until It's Over

Here's one of our favorite blind date stories. A few years ago, Chris and Brad coincidentally had arranged blind dates on the same night. Chris, who was not yet living in Manhattan, went to Brad's apartment to get ready for his date. Chris and Brad discussed where each of them was going and made a plan to meet afterward if their blind dates didn't work out. So off they went—Chris to a fancy uptown restaurant, Brad to a downtown bar.

About halfway through Chris's dinner, Brad showed up at the restaurant alone. His date and he hadn't hit it off. He pulled up a chair and told Chris and his date all about it. Chris began to notice that his date seemed very interested in Brad's story—and in Brad. The chemistry was not there between Chris and this woman, so it didn't bother him at all. In fact, Chris found it rather comical.

After dinner, the three of them made their way to the bar. (Chris was basically a bystander at this point.) Brad and Chris's date began to talk, laugh, and get very drunk together. Chris wound up leaving the two of them behind and going home. Brad, now on his second blind date of the night, made the most of it—he wound up back at her apartment that evening for a crazy night together.

This one just goes to show that you can never predict how a date will end. Chris and his date didn't strike a match, but she hit it off with Brad. If she was out for fun, she certainly found it as a "good for now" girl. If she was looking for Mr. Right, she didn't play her cards right by making the first night such a wild one. No woman who sleeps with a guy on the first night is going to be put in his "marriage material" girl category. Keep this in mind.

What Can a Woman Do to Make a Blind Date One He Will Never Forget?

The Call

Well, let's start off with the phone call. A guy reads a lot into this first contact. If making a call seems like no big deal to you, imagine how we feel during a conversation like this one:

CHRIS: Hi, this is Chris.

BLIND DATE: Chris . . . Chris who?

CHRIS: You know, Lisa's sister's cousin's friend from college who knows your boss.

We can't understand why women give their phone numbers out to their friends in order to get set up on a blind date, and then act as if they have no idea who the guy is when he calls. Come on, ladies—make it a little easier on a man. Try to sound like you know exactly who your blind date is when he calls. Be sure to tell him how glad you are that he called and that you've heard good things about him from your friend. Understand how stressful it is for him to make that call and sound enthusiastic and excited in your conversation with him. You will put him at ease right away, which can only lead to a more relaxed conversation that will score you huge points with him right off the bat.

You Meet

Okay, the day has arrived for your blind date to take place. What's next? Well, as we've said, looks are big this first night out. You'll either have the look your date wants or you won't. There isn't much you can do about your height, hair color, weight, or complexion. But you can radiate an outward glow that most men would find hard to resist. You can do this by feeling good about yourself and showing it with an aura of confidence, good humor, and optimism. If you can't meet a blind date with genuine good feelings, if you are faking it or in a bad humor, you are probably better off canceling. If you go, go to the door or the lobby on time and in good spirits. Greet your date with a handshake and your best smile. Try to give him a compliment and accept any nice comments he has for you graciously.

The Comment That Can Blow It All

So now you have met your blind date. The first awkward moment is finally behind you. You are each assessing the other's looks and considering if they meet approval. You are on your way. *Stop right there*—it is at this point that the most common mistake is made. To break the ice or to simply protect themselves, many women say something along the lines of "I can't believe I'm on a blind date, I never do this" or "I didn't even really want to do this but my friend made me." These statements do nothing to alleviate the embarrassment or discomfort the two of you are feeling. In fact, blurting out lines like these can make the situation even more awkward and put the two of you on a downhill slide before the date has even started. Instead, look right into your date's eyes and say something like, "I'm so glad to finally meet you." Imagine how quickly that will take the edge off his nervousness and how comfortable you will make your date feel.

At the Restaurant or Bar

This is your chance to get to know each other and give your date some insight into you that goes beyond your appearance. So, answer his questions and ask him about himself. Keep the conversation flowing. If you discover a topic of interest you share, explore that. Focus all of your attention on him; don't let your eyes wander around the room. Laugh at his jokes and flirt. If he suggests dinner to follow the drinks you had planned or coffee after dinner, take him up on it if you like him and are still looking to make this a memorable date. Don't drink too much and don't insist on paying the bill if he picks it up and wants to pay. Let him take the lead.

What to Do If He's Rude

Some people don't know how to behave on blind dates. We've heard of guys showing up drunk, grabbing a blind date's behind as they walk out of her building, making rude comments to the waiter, and flirting with another woman at the bar they go to for drinks. If a blind date acts inappropriately or disrespectfully, end the date immediately. Be firm and direct. Don't give the guy a speech, just say that you are interested in meeting someone nice and will not stand for such behavior. Tell him the two of you should part ways with no hard feelings.

The End of the Evening

You usually know by the end of a first date if you want to see the other person again. If you do, make it clear with your parting comments and full lingering eye contact that you'd like to see this guy again. Part with a hug or a quick kiss if you feel so inclined. Even if you want to, don't go to his place for a nightcap or invite him up to yours. You'll kill any chances for the long term if you do.

The Blind Date Dream-Come-True

We told you earlier that Sandra set Brad up on a very successful blind date. You know we couldn't leave it at that. We wanted to wait and use Brad's story and a few others here to drive home the fact that blind dates really can work. Your friends can be the ones to introduce you to Mr. Right.

Brad was set up with his wife, Cheryl. It was a date he will never forget. It began like any blind date. Brad was excited, hoping to meet the perfect girl. He picked up Cheryl at her apartment and immediately noticed that she was a tall, beautiful, and stylishly dressed young woman. They went to an outdoor café in Manhattan and enjoyed a fun and lighthearted conversation. They spoke about their likes and dislikes, including traveling, the beach, and many other topics. Throughout the date Brad knew that he wanted to see Cheryl again very soon. When they left the café they walked back toward Cheryl's apartment. At some point Brad and Cheryl found that they'd walked around her block about five times, lost in conversation. They left each other with a small kiss. Brad went home and tried to hold himself back from calling her immediately.

Alison and George had both been told by mutual friends how perfect they'd be for each other. When they met Alison was twenty-five and working for a clothing designer and distributor in Queens and George, twenty-eight, was a communications consultant for a multinational corporation. Alison says when she opened the door and saw George standing there on the front steps she knew that he was "the one." George loved the smile that Alison beamed at him from the moment they said hello. They went out to dinner that night at an Italian restaurant overlooking Long Island Sound.

They laughed and talked about their families and their work and their hopes for the future. The next day they both told the friends who had introduced them they felt as though they had found their soul mate.

But they didn't rush things. They dated each other for a year before George moved in with Alison. George got a new job and traveled a lot. Alison got used to his business schedule and cultivated her own interests in decorating and painting to keep her busy. They got to know each other's habits, moods, and tastes. On the two-year anniversary of that first blind date, Alison came home for lunch to find a trail of posters, each one with a single word on it, running from the front door to the bedroom. They read, "You are the most loving and beautiful woman I have ever met. Will you please be my wife?" By then she was in tears. George burst out from the closet to give his fiancée a big hug. They were married the following June and now, three years later, are the proud parents of two boys.

Abbey and Charles almost didn't meet at all. Abbey's mom was a relentless matchmaker, and Abbey was irritated when her mother said she had someone for her to meet. Abbey, a twenty-eight-year-old magazine writer, felt she could find her own man and took her mother's overzealous behavior as a lack of confidence in her. But one weekend Abbey was depressed that her calendar showed two whole months of free Saturday nights. When her mother brought up her single, cute cardiologist for the tenth time, Abbey's resolve buckled and she agreed to meet him.

Charles called Abbey and they arranged a date for the following Friday. The two had agreed to go to dinner and then a hockey game, since they were both fans of a local team. Abbey thought Charles sounded charming on the phone and was curious about him. Charles said later that Abbey's sharp wit and confidence in their first conversation got his attention right away. Charles turned up in a black convertible sports car carrying a huge bouquet of roses. Abbey was speechless and somewhat guarded since Charles seemed slick and a little too good to be true. Charles drove them through the back roads to a small restaurant he liked. He talked about his love of the country and how glad he was to have his farmhouse retreat outside of the city. Abbey asked him about his dogs and his work, his family and his past. As the evening went on, Charles seemed more genuine to her and she let her guard down. Abbey told him that she, too, loved the country and her favorite activity was gardening. They left the quiet dining room to go to the hockey game and there they both screamed until they were hoarse. Their team won.

Charles was very attracted to Abbey and it was for this very reason he hesitated before calling her again. He knew if he did it would be the end of his dating days. Just when Abbey was sure she'd never hear from him again, Charles called. She pretended it was no big deal that she hadn't heard from him in a month, though when they went out on their second date they both felt the sparks flying. Charles shared his reason for not calling sooner with Abbey and from then on he didn't let a week go by without seeing her. After dating for a year, Charles proposed. To Abbey's mom's delight the couple got married in her dooryard garden in July among a small group of family and friends.

If you accept those blind dates, this could happen to you!

On-line Dating

Meeting on-line has become a much more viable and acceptable way to find a date than it was just a few years ago. We

know that some people are embarrassed about meeting people in chat rooms, through on-line dating services, or on
message boards. If you think about it, using a chat room is
not that much different than going to a bar to try to meet
someone. Talking on-line is not unlike talking in person. We
can't figure out why there is a stigma attached to on-line
methods of meeting women. We find the Internet a great
new resource for those looking for Mr. Right. In fact, we
recommend it and hope that soon women won't be ashamed
to log on and see this as a very cool way to meet guys.

Why? We feel that there is the potential to meet someone
faster and move the relationship to a more personal level
when it starts on-line. We know for a fact that men use on-
line dating services to try to meet someone expeditiously. For
professional men with busy schedules, the traditional meeting venues—bars, clubs, etc.—are often hard to get to. In
contrast, they never have to leave their offices to meet
women on-line. What could be easier or faster? In some
ways, it's no different than arranging a blind date. Instead of
being set up by a friend, you're essentially setting up yourself.

It's Not Perfect

There are definite downsides to on-line dating we must
point out. On-line dating can lead to endless e-mails that
don't go anywhere. Or, if they do go somewhere, it often
takes forever. Sometimes you have to wait so long for a
response that it's like dating through the U.S. Postal Service.
The man writes an e-mail. Five days later the woman finally
writes back. The man responds, and then a week passes
before he receives her reply. It's as if a man asks the woman a
question, and she leaves the room and then comes back a

week later with an answer. This can be very tiresome, frustrating, and an all-around big hassle for a professional man.

Second, women are often very distrustful about the man with whom they're corresponding—and won't give out any information at all. This makes the man feel as if she thinks he's a molester or worse. We understand that some caution is necessary. When a man is trying to get to know a woman, she has to be somewhat forthcoming or a date is never going to materialize.

And third, when it comes to e-mail, there is way too much overanalysis. Women tend to analyze every word a man writes. Things that don't typically matter suddenly matter a lot. When a man meets a woman at a bar, his spelling skills are rarely an issue. But on-line, a woman assumes all sorts of things about a man simply because he uses incorrect grammar or makes a typo. The least spontaneous method is the message board—that's where people get super analytical, trying to read too much into things ("He wrote in all lowercase letters? He must be lazy!"). Sometimes on-line dating seems very superficial, based too much on profiles, writing, and typing skills—and not on one's true personality.

Improving Your Chances of an On-line Connection

We know that there are many professional guys like us logging on to find Ms. Right. Here's how you can get and keep their attention:

- Your best bet to meet a guy is a chat room. In our experience, chat rooms are the most spontaneous method of communicating on-line and give rise to what feels like a real, natural conversation. But some people we know have also had luck with on-line dating services and posting personal ads on the Web.

• Try to respond quickly to any e-mails you receive. You don't want to waste his time—or yours.

• Include a photo of yourself with your profile, if possible. Or, offer to send one along electronically or through the mail to guys with whom you strike up a promising correspondence on-line. Seeing what you look like will quell many men's fears about meeting you and may move the relationship more quickly to the stage where you meet. A visual can reveal to others that you are not their type—saving you both from investing any more time in your correspondence.

• If he doesn't want to meet you, don't take it personally. As with any dating scenario, on-line dating is an opportunity to get to know someone. The chances that each and every encounter will have a fairy-tale ending are very slim. Sometimes he won't want to get together, and vice versa. The important thing to remember is that dating on-line offers you another way to get to know people you otherwise might never meet.

• When it comes to the content of his e-mails, try to put things in perspective. If he's made a mistake or two, keep an open mind and realize that just because someone misspells a word, it doesn't mean he can't be the man of your dreams. Informal notes are by no means a fair or complete representation of a professional man.

• Recognize that it's difficult to get the true essence of someone from a phone conversation or an exchange of e-mails.

It's best to meet him in person. Treat your on-line dating like traditional dating. At a certain point you've got to meet.

• Don't let the e-mail exchange develop too far or go on too long. It's like having two-hour phone conversations before a blind date. A big no-no. Believe us—it's a terrible feeling to have shared a lot of personal information with someone only to find out she is a total freak. Save the regrets by keeping the pre-date correspondence to a minimum. After five e-mails or a chat room, cut it off and set a face-to-face date. Putting off meeting in person at this point can be a major strain for the man. Remember, he wants to move the relationship along. And so do you. So why keep things at a slow pace with e-mail when you could make things much more natural by meeting in person—and really getting to know this guy?

• After you've exchanged five e-mails maximum (and he seems like a good guy) agree to meet your e-date in a public area. If scheduling via e-mail becomes a problem, give him your phone number. This may be old-fashioned, but it's often more efficient.

• Take safety precautions when you meet your e-date for the first time. Don't meet him at 11 P.M. on a Sunday night in the park. Plan to meet in a public place surrounded by other people and always tell a friend or two where and when you are going. If this approach still leaves you uncomfortable, the safest suggestion would be to arrange for each of you to bring along a friend. This may sound extreme to you, but we know people who won't have a first e-date any other way. They just are not comfortable going alone to meet a person with whom they've only corresponded.

- Consider on-line dating like a blind date—the only difference is that you're setting yourself up. You have to be willing to take chances and be adventurous. You also have to put your best foot forward—be optimistic, friendly, and confident.

Dating Players (or Ex-Players)

Sure women have dated more than one person at a time, but they all told us they never felt as if they were juggling men. Conversely, men do date more than one woman for longer periods of time for the pure excitement that "juggling women" provides. Guys like these are often known as players. A man plays the field because it is an ego boost, it is an exciting challenge. Being wanted and liked by many women makes him feel good. You might think that there's an insecurity issue here and maybe that is the case. Hey, we are the first to admit that guys are insecure when it comes to women. But we believe that a player often sees many women just because it makes sense and is fun.

As far as a guy is concerned, dating more than one woman is a win-win situation. Think about it. A man has the chance to sleep with more than one woman and he is also giving himself the opportunity to meet Ms. Right. We know it isn't fair to women, and oftentimes it is done with total disregard for a woman's feelings. Dating several women simultaneously is totally selfish and is satisfying only the needs of a man. So how is this information valuable to you as a woman? We feel very strongly that knowing more about men will inevitably help you understand them better. It will allow you to have more successful relationships with men and recognize the type of relationship that has no future, in which case it's time to exit stage left.

As you might suspect, a guy in the juggling mode is often not Mr. Right. Players are enjoying the thrill, excitement, and variety of dating many women. They are having fun, having sex, and getting their egos stroked. A man's head can really swell up when he is on a roll with many different women. He starts to feel as if he's the best-looking movie star in the world and nobody can stop him. It's a great feeling, a difficult one to give up.

But here's the good news. Most men will do anything to keep the right woman in their lives once they meet her. If he happens to meet Ms. Right while he is in "juggling mode," a guy will immediately consider letting go of a bunch of "good for now" girls to spend time with her. Pretty soon the shallow dating life he has been leading will be much less important to him than trying to foster a long-term relationship with his "marriage material" girl.

This transition doesn't come easy, especially for men who are dating many great women. Once men are in this mode, they feel that they can land anyone. They get caught in the illusion that there's always someone better out there. By staying with this woman or with that woman, they are missing out on being with the next one, who is even better. It sounds crazy, but it's true. Just take a look at some celebrities—famous athletes, musicians or, of course, actors. They always have a hot woman around them and their relationships always seem to start off great. But they never last. They always wind up in terrible breakups. We're sure that the breakups are no worse than what we non-celebs go through. It's just that the famous people's lives are sensationalized and plastered all over the media. We still find it baffling that there are men out there who seem to get tired of sleeping with Cindy Crawford or Pamela Anderson or Gwyneth Paltrow. But it goes to prove the point—men often think there's someone better out there and that they are missing out. Men tend to look at juggling women as an art form that takes skill and practice.

The True Story Behind This Juggling Act

What are men thinking and feeling as they are juggling women? First, please realize that the women men juggle are never considered "marriage material" girls—they will always be "good for now" girls. A man feels absolutely no sense of commitment to any of these women. He is in a casual dating and casual sex mode. The great benefit the player enjoys is being free. Since he doesn't have any sense of commitment to the women he sees he feels no need to explain to anyone where he is or what he's doing. Cocky fellow that he is, a man is usually shameless about flaunting the fact that he has a virtual harem in front of anyone—even those women he's seeing. He enjoys flirting with another woman on the phone or playing provocative answering machine messages for a female audience. Since he doesn't have serious feelings for these women, it is totally acceptable to show off or at least not hide what he's up to.

Though this is exactly how players think and feel, you will never get a man to tell you any of this information straight out in some "relationship" conversation. He will dodge and avoid any topics that smack of commitment and tell you what you want to hear just to keep you on his active list. He won't be asking you to explain what you do with the six other nights you're not seeing him, either. Most men who are juggling women do not care if a woman is seeing other guys and getting action elsewhere. Additionally, he wouldn't lose any sleep if you left him. In fact, he'd rather have you leave than ask him to change. He would just view your departure as another night opened up to date someone else.

You Can't Force a Player to Change

A friend of ours was once juggling several women at one time. Looking back, it was clear to us that he wasn't interested in these women for a long-term commitment. He didn't spend much time with them, he didn't ask them about the important things going on in their lives, and he spent a lot of time away from them, out with his friends—trying to meet other women, of course.

The women were oblivious to all the signals he was sending. One woman foolishly demanded more from him. After asking him to change his ways several times, she announced that she was going to do the same thing that he was doing. She was going to go out with her friends more and wasn't going to turn down dates with other men. From what we could see, she was testing our friend to see if he would come around and stop playing games with her.

This woman made the mistake most women we know make. She sacrificed her happiness by incorrectly assuming that she would change him. Since he didn't really have any feelings for her, he was not fazed by her "threats." In fact, he felt as though she was giving him just what he wanted: less responsibility and more freedom. This woman's tactics backfired. She would have been wise to recognize she was one of many women our friend considered "good for now" and would never make it into his "wife potential" category. Then she would have seen that she really had no leverage. If she wasn't happy with this guy's behavior, her only smart option would be to stop seeing him. She was not going to change him.

Seriously Dating Yesterday's Player

We do want to caution women about a guy who has been known to be a player who suddenly meets a woman he thinks is Ms. Right and cuts off all of his ties to other women. A guy who makes a drastic move like this can either be falling in love, which is a great thing, or has just convinced himself that he wants a change of pace. This is where danger lies. A guy who jumps into a serious relationship, straight from being a player, may be doing it for the wrong reasons. He may have put his needs and requirements for a lifetime companion second to his desire to get out of the dating world. In fact, a guy may not even be conscious of the fact that he has done this.

Some might say a guy is "settling" for a woman who happens to be around at the time he gets the urge to have only one woman in his life, others might say the man simply doesn't know what he wants in a woman. In either case, this is extremely dangerous for you, because it's difficult for a woman to spot a guy in this dilemma. If a player has become bored with the dating scene and is looking to settle down, he will appear to be Prince Charming. Unless you are the right woman for him, ultimately your relationship will fail.

So what can a woman looking for commitment do? If you suspect your guy has just jumped out of the player mode and into your arms, put the brakes on and slow things down. It is fine for you to enjoy the "Don Juan" approach with which most guys start serious dating, but it is more important for you to find out quickly Don Juan's motivation. You must evaluate if his feelings for you are sincere or if he is just enjoying the novelty of a relationship that goes beyond casual sex. Assess what stage of his career he is in and gauge the seriousness of his commitment to you.

In most cases, the man will not be so straightforward with you on this latter point. Not because he is trying to deceive you in any way—it might be something about which he isn't even aware. He might think he's totally in love with you and not even realize that his strong reaction has come from a change in lifestyle rather than his actual feelings about you.

One way to test your man's true feelings, even if he isn't clear about them himself, is to go out on dates with him to places that are usually known as singles spots. Couples who are truly in love can go out to these places and have a great time together. If your man is totally and completely into you and your relationship, it won't matter much to him where he is. He'll follow you anywhere and be completely focused on you. He wouldn't notice if you sat down next to a table of supermodels. In the early stages of love, your man will be looking at you, talking about you, and doing all it takes to make you happy.

If you have an ex-player on your hands who is just fed up with the dating scene, we guarantee he will be much more attuned to the surroundings in the singles spots than he will to what you are saying, doing, or wearing. Usually, he will take the scene in and make fun of the other guys trying to hook up and the desperado women searching for their future husbands. Even though he can't take his eyes off the crowd, he may make reference to the fact that he feels so lucky that he has found you and is not in that scene any-more. Look at his actions, don't be taken in just by words. If your guy exhibits a roving eye and has trouble focusing on you, we'd say any long-term potential with him is a long shot. Drop him.

Once Chris brought his then-girlfriend to a friend's birthday party at a trendy bar. Since he was in a happy relationship, the bar scene didn't hold any real interest for Chris. It didn't matter to him where he was. Chris hadn't seen his friend in a while and was looking forward to meeting up with him and the rest of the crew. Having dated his girlfriend for eight months at that point, Chris hadn't been out to the bars and nightclubs in quite a while. After being harassed at the door by the bouncer, Chris and his date were "allowed" the privilege of entering this dark, loud, crowded watering hole for twenty dollars each.

It only took a matter of seconds for Chris to realize that he was right back in the meat market. Guys were drinking themselves into oblivion, spending money, and gawking at the women. In his happy and committed relationship, Chris felt as though he had just entered a foreign country—and was happy about that. This kind of scene was no longer appealing because of his healthy relationship. (Of course, now that Chris is single, he likes to visit bars and clubs in hopes of meeting Ms. Right.)

Accusing Him of Being a Player

Even if you are trying to find out if your man is tired of the dating scene or if he is sincerely in love with you, it's definitely not a good idea to confront him directly about his recent player status—not if you have any hopes for a future with him.

We have seen many promising relationships fail because women call men "players" or tell them that they have a reputation as a player. We can't figure out why a woman would do such a thing with a man she is interested in for the long term. If a man truly loves a woman and she is accusing him of being interested in her merely as a sexual conquest, he will feel defeated and frustrated. He may believe that she will never really trust him. Whether he was a player or not, a man will feel that a woman who brings up this issue has such a strong preconceived notion about his past (and possibly present) activities that he will have no way to convince her his history is irrelevant now that he has met her. That is a very frustrating spot to be in, especially if you are with a woman for whom you have growing feelings.

If a promising Mr. Right raises a similar question about your having a past marked by a string of sexual conquests, take this as a red flag that you aren't a "marriage material" girl for him. Whether you were a player or not should not matter to him if he is in love with you. Of course, there are exceptions to every rule. Pay close attention to the conversation that follows when he raises this issue. Does he sound as if he's trusting you more as you reassure him of your good intentions? Or, is he fearful no matter what you say? Take a look below at how Chris handled such an accusation— notice he doesn't get defensive or make excuses for his past. You shouldn't either. Your actions in a relationship should speak for themselves. Your date should not be concerned with how other people said you've acted in previous relationships; he should pay attention only to what you are like with him.

Chris can remember meeting a woman he was very attracted to from the first date. She had the same feelings for him. They enjoyed each other's company immensely, and they spent a lot of time together soon after they started dating. As time passed, they both realized they had very significant feelings for each other (and with these came mutual feelings of vulnerability). They both got quite serious about the other very quickly. The relationship held great potential.

One night after a romantic dinner and a great time together, this woman expressed some of her concerns about her feelings with Chris. She told him that she knew some people who had heard that Chris was interested in women as sexual conquests alone and she was concerned that this was what she was for him. She liked him and didn't want to get hurt, so she felt the need to raise the issue, even though Chris had been the perfect gentleman in the relationship with her and seemed to genuinely enjoy the time they spent together.

Chris's feelings for this woman were sincere. He had shown her that by spending a great deal of time with her. He had taken her out for expensive dinners, bought her flowers, and told her how she was different from other women he had met. When she mentioned her fears about Chris being a player, he was absolutely devastated. He understood that his reputation had preceded him and that it was causing this woman a great deal of concern. He told her as much and assured her that she had nothing to worry about. He told her that she was special in his eyes and he had hoped that they would have the chance to spend a great deal of time together.

In spite of Chris's attempts to reassure her, his date seemed to get more distant as the conversation went on. By the end of the evening, Chris felt this woman he cared deeply for was trying to protect herself from being hurt and couldn't open up to him. In his mind, Chris had two-and-a-half strikes against him in his relationship with her. He felt that there would be nothing he could say or do to help her ever to get over her fear. After all, she had told him that she found it very difficult to trust him even though he had done nothing to her to deserve this. He wasn't "playing" her at all, yet she feared that he was, just because of what she had heard about him.

Chris immediately felt this woman he really liked dismissed his sincere attentions as manipulative tactics to try to get her into bed. This was a terrible way for a relationship to start. Chris figured if she still had these concerns after all they had experienced together, she would never be able to trust him no matter what he said or did. The relationship was never the same after this talk, and soon Chris and this woman stopped seeing one another.

We hate to see good relationships fail because women just don't understand how men think, feel, and act. Please heed our advice and don't let a man's past interfere with your feelings for him or his feelings for you. Get to know your man and make your own judgments about him from his actions *with you*.

So, yes, in general men known for their singular interest in getting a woman into bed can mean trouble—and should be avoided. But be aware that men who were once players can become great boyfriends—and husbands. Just look at Brad—talk about a transformed player! Do not allow a man's past reputation rule out a relationship with him. Yes, it's important to be cautious and use good judgment, but at the same time try to have an open mind and realize that men do grow out of certain phases—especially when the right woman comes along.

Fast-Starting Relationships

Have you ever found yourself in a relationship where you got completely swept off your feet right from the word hello? Although love at first sight is very romantic, it just isn't realistic. Sure there are healthy marriages here and there that seemed to have come together naturally after a short courtship and been great successes. Sometimes, two people meet and are just meant to be together right from the start, but these situations are rare. More realistically, love and relationships need to develop. People need time to get to know each other, especially people who expect to spend the rest of their lives together. Let's face it, marriage is forever—and forever is a long time. There's no need to rush into things.

We're not saying that a passionate connection can't blossom into a long-term love. It can. You just have to be aware of what's happening in the heat of an intense relationship and take steps to preserve what you have found.

Our friend Jane met Eddie at a company Christmas party. He was a consultant with the public relations firm where she worked. He asked her to dance and Jane felt a spark from the moment she looked into his dark brown eyes. They spent the night dancing under the lights and talking in the shadows. They were one of the last couples to leave the party, and afterward they went out for a drink at the bar next door. They didn't want to say good-bye. During the weeks that followed Jane and Eddie talked to each other every day on the telephone and went out every night. They had sex after knowing each other just seven days—it was great and just made them more crazy about each other.

But, within that first month, Jane and Eddie both realized what they felt for each other was very different than anything either of them had experienced before. They didn't want that flame they had to burn out. So, they consciously made a point to limit their dates to two or three a week. In between they saw other friends, went to the gym, and worked. As hard as this was at first, these two knew slowing down their pace a bit would help them maintain their own identities in the rush of love. Eddie's and Jane's ability to trust that their relationship would develop gradually—and to trust that their love would remain alive—helped them build a strong foundation for their future together. They dated for three years and then got married. This year their first child is on the way.

We have found that women in our society (and, in some cases, men) feel obligated to live their lives based on a time line. You go to high school, graduate, go to college, graduate, play around in your early twenties, and then get married in your late twenties or early thirties. Wanting to adhere to this perceived schedule is a common reason for people to marry when they are not truly in love. Whether it's panic that sets in because they feel they are never going to find a spouse, or because their biological clock is ticking, many, many marriages seem to take place out of pure convenience or preconceived expectations about the right age to marry. This is especially true with women we know who've crossed the "thirty-year-old time line." These women seem extremely insecure and in a tremendous hurry to get married. So much so that they sacrifice their true feelings and needs in order to land a husband.

Oftentimes these relationships fall into the "fast-start, fast-end" category. Men and women meet each other and, based on the time and place they are at in their lives, they feel as if marriage is the next expected step, so they get on the express train to the altar from day one. These relationships are riddled with unnecessary pain and wasted time. Ultimately, fast-start relationships fizzle out just as quickly as they start. When they end, they leave a trail of broken plans and dreams in their wake. Usually men and women in these fast-start, fast-end scenarios fall in love with the excitement of a new relationship and propel commitment along at warp speed. Their mad dash might include moving in together, talking about getting engaged and married, meeting the families, etc., in the first few weeks or months of their relationship. All the while the couple has forgotten to focus on what is most important to a healthy long-term union—how they feel about one another and getting to know this person with whom they might want to share their lives.

One day, a few months into their frenzied romance, these two people wake up and, if they're lucky, realize that they don't know enough about each other to make a decision to spend their lives together. Either they bail out then or they slow down and proceed at a reasonable speed. Other times, the unlucky ones either fail to wake up and notice they have chosen the wrong person, but rationalize their feelings and stay in the relationship anyway. These relationships are destined for long-term unhappiness or failure.

The Fast-Start, Fast-End Guy

So, who is the guy in the fast-start, fast-end relationship? He is probably a man who is falling in love with the idea of being in a relationship. He is also probably a guy who is coming off a long drought and hasn't been with a woman in a while. He may also be a man on the rebound. In the latter case, the fast-start relationship is a way for him to get back into his comfort zone of having a serious girlfriend again. In any case, this guy has made an irrational and rushed decision to dive into commitment. He hasn't focused on the woman he's with. He doesn't know her traits and characteristics and if they match those that he needs to make him happy down the road. All he knows is that he feels good now. He has no clue what the future holds.

We think that the odds of these fast-start relationships working out in the long run are extremely low. The best way we can articulate our reasons why this is so, is to compare getting involved in a long term, committed monogamous relationship to certain major decisions and tasks that we are subjected to in our professional careers. In our jobs, we professional men are usually making key decisions on a daily basis as we work our way to the top of the career ladder. Before making a decision, we want to take time to collect all the information we can. After surveying it all, we decide. This is a reflexive process; it's just the nature of how we go about our responsibilities in our day-to-day professional lives.

This process spills over into our personal lives. We rarely make a serious commitment without long, drawn-out observation and thought. And to be honest, the decision to marry someone may be one of the biggest we have had to make at this point in our lives. We are not going to rush into it. It's just not the way we operate. Especially since it is also a decision that we have to make with little guidance and absolutely no history or experience behind us. We have to collect all the data ourselves and be confident that this woman is "the one" before we tie the knot that binds us to her for life. This means our decision-making process is even more calculated and more deliberate than it is with lesser issues. You've bought this book to see why we won't move toward commitment and marriage a little faster, right?

Looking at the situation this way, we have come to the conclusion that the fast-start relationship guy is a man who is not in his right mind. He gets involved fast for the wrong reasons. He certainly hasn't had ample time to get to know the woman to whom he wants to commit or to analyze the change of life he is proposing. As we see it, he has made a decision based on a fantasy he has in his head about the woman he is with and the relationship they will have, not reality.

The Story on Fast-Start, Fast-End Relationships

So why would a man get involved in a fast-start, fast-end relationship? He could be caught up in the moment. Things can appear to be very exciting and promising in the beginning of many relationships. If he hasn't had sex in a while, having a fast-start relationship may be very appealing to him. If he was previously in a long-term relationship with plans of engagement that broke off, he might be looking for a replacement to help him get back to that comfortable point in his life. What stage a man is in his career can also determine the likelihood of him becoming Mr. Fast-Start. If he is in the Successful Stage, for example, he may be impatient for a longer-term commitment and may feel with all his years focused on work that he is behind in the process of finding a spouse. If a woman comes along with whom he feels very comfortable, he might not hesitate to fast forward to commitment.

As we've seen, pushing a relationship into warp speed is completely contradictory to the way a normal man is used to making decisions. Men are very calculated in their decision-making process and need to gather all the facts and analyze all the options before making a move. However, men are human and they certainly feel good when they meet someone they like and at least *think* they are falling in love with.

So they just get caught up in that comfortable feeling and make the mistake of going down a fast track with someone they barely know. While it's almost guaranteed that these types of relationships don't last too long and end painfully—either with a lot of hurt feelings or even worse for those who make the mistake of marrying the person, in divorce court—they happen quite often. So we really want to caution women against their natural instincts to get into these relationships that seem so romantic in the beginning. These types of relationships are usually products of infatuations. People in them are falling in love for the sake of falling in love, rather than genuinely bonding with another person.

If you still aren't convinced that commitment on the rush plan should be avoided, read this real-life example we witnessed of a fast-start relationship that ended just as quickly as it began. A female friend of ours met a Wall Street attorney with a large apartment, a brand-new Porsche convertible, and a thick wallet. They hit it off immediately and became inseparable right away. In just two short weeks, they were spending every free moment they had together. They were both feeling they had found "the one"—that person they would spend the rest of their lives loving. Their connection to each other felt natural to each of them, and they had a great time together.

We were out to dinner with our friend one night, and she was simply glowing with happiness. She told us she truly felt in love with her newfound man. She felt so strongly about her relationship that she was adamant with us that this was a special fast-start case. She admitted to us that they were saying they loved each other inside of two weeks. She also indicated that although they were spending every moment together and they were sleeping at each other's apartments every night, he was being a complete gentleman and they had not had sex through all of this. Though she conceded that the relationship seemed too good to be true, our friend said she deserved a dream man after all of the guys she had dated who would never commit.

This just didn't seem right to us. We cautioned our friend about situations like this and told her that she needed to slow things down and really get to know him better. We stuck to our guns and advised her to back off some and ease into this relationship. However, our friend refused to listen to us. She continued to enjoy the relationship as this man sent her gourmet breakfast by delivery and had car service available to take her wherever she wanted to go. He was truly a charmer, and she was loving it. In fact, our friend and her new love even got engaged.

Did we panic and think we were wrong? No way—we still stuck to our opinions. The three of us felt this relationship had just gone too far too fast and was destined for failure. Sure enough, our friend left this guy just a few short months into the engagement. As they spent more time together, she finally understood that they had never really got to know each other. They clashed when he started talking about work and how he felt no remorse crushing small companies for his large corporate client. Our friend soon realized that she would characterize this guy as a barracuda-type attorney who had no compassion. His behavior at work repulsed her. When the true colors of this man she was engaged to emerged, our friend determined that they weren't made for each other at all. She told us that he was completely shocked by the turn of events and heartbroken that his fiancée had left him. At least one of them woke up before they said "I do."

Danger Signs of a Fast-Start, Fast-End Relationship

- He tells you he loves you within the first few months.
- He sleeps over every night within the first two months.
- He wants you to move in prior to six months.
- He discusses marriage prior to a year.

What Can You Do?

Now, don't worry if you are currently very interested in a man with whom you became involved very quickly. Fast-start relationships can work out, but once you recognize your relationship as one that got serious quickly, you must take the necessary steps to slow things down. Sure, there's love at first sight and all of the special chemistry that comes between two people who are just meant to be together. If all these strong feelings are in a relationship right from the start, that's wonderful. But why rush things? If your initial feelings are real, true, and sincere, they will be even stronger in the future. We guarantee that fast-start relationships that aren't slowed to a more normal pace will always end in heartache, whereas relationships that are taken at a nice, easy pace have a much better chance of bringing true happiness to both partners.

How do you slow this thing down? Start by talking. We feel that you should bring up the topic of your fast-start relationship. Discuss with your man in straightforward terms your desire to keep your connection strong while taking the time to get better acquainted. It sounds very simple, and it can be. Start by telling your boyfriend how great things are, how happy you are, and how much you enjoy talking about your future together. Then reinforce your thoughts by telling him that you really want to give this relationship a fighting chance, and the only way to do that is to slow things down a bit and really get to know each other on a much deeper level.

We think men would react well to this approach because it is so practical. It is something they can relate to in their everyday lives; especially at work, where men take things slowly, making decisions deliberately after considering all aspects of a situation. What man wouldn't respond positively to this approach? By convincing yourself that the relationship will be destined for failure if it continues rocketing ahead, you will be taking the first step to a longer-lasting, successful relationship. Bringing your expectations back down to earth and looking at your interaction more realistically is the only way that fast-start relationships have a chance of not becoming fast-end relationships.

We can't stress enough that if you feel that you're in a fast-start relationship, it's imperative that you slow things down. As hard as it may be, you need to set some boundaries in order to protect yourself and your future together. If it's the beginning of the relationship, tell him he can sleep over only once a week. If he's telling you that he loves you sooner than you think is natural, then tell him so. If he's pressuring you to move in with him before you're ready, then you're going to have to share your feelings and concerns with him. Remember, for the long-term relationship it's best that things develop slowly and naturally.

Dating Coworkers

We have received thousands of letters and e-mails asking us to talk about office romances and whether or not they are good bets that will evolve into long, committed relationships. First, there are a host of social issues as well as rules your company may enforce about office dating. You must understand what your company policy is before you make a decision to date someone at work.

If your employer doesn't allow dating between coworkers, then obviously you risk a great deal by doing so. Even if dating is allowed in your workplace, some men may have a personal rule about not mixing business with pleasure. As we've mentioned before, a man's career is very, very important to him. He will be extremely cautious about doing anything that could possibly jeopardize all the years of hard work he has put in to get where he is in his professional life. Understand that it's a very serious decision for a man to date a woman who works with him.

Professional men are so caught up in the importance of their career that they may not even be open to the possibility of dating a woman at work. The fear of losing his job or being accused of some kind of sexual harassment may just be enough for a professional man to avoid any potentially threatening situations. No matter what happens, any accusation of sexual harassment is a lose-lose proposition. Guilty or not, a man's career can be finished even with one false accusation. So men are extremely cautious when it comes to dating someone at the office.

Why Men Risk the Dangers of Dating on the Job

You might ask, if a man's career is so important to him why would any guy even entertain introducing another risk by getting romantically involved with a coworker? That's a good question and will help us make our point very clearly. Professional men who work long, hard hours have very little time for a meaningful social life. In today's fast-paced society, career-oriented professionals seem to have a harder and harder time meeting a person with whom they would consider sharing a life. Marriages are happening later in life compared with our parents' and grandparents' generations and men and women have to put in longer hours in order to become successful at work. In many cases today, the work environment provides dedicated professionals with social lives. Since professional men spend so much time with coworkers and don't really have much time to pursue an active social life outside the office, they wind up socializing with people at work. Dangerous or not, dating a colleague seems like the natural next step.

As the president of the United States has proven, men may go with the flow and get involved with women with whom they work, whether it's a good idea or not. It's difficult to be around someone every day to whom you are attracted and with whom you get along well and not follow your natural instincts to take the relationship farther. If there's chemistry between a man and a woman, it will grow as they spend more time together, even if it's all in the office. Besides, a man feels confident at work, where his true strengths and talents are being showcased to a woman in whom he is interested. Think about it—a man would never be afforded the opportunity of having a woman see how well he performs professionally if he met her at a bar or on a blind date. The work environment provides a unique place for both the man and the woman to get to see the attributes of each other in their careers. It can be very attractive to see someone in action at his or her job.

For a man who dates a woman at work, most of the groundwork is already done. This is a very positive point that can outweigh the dangers that come from interoffice romance. The professional man gets to know people at work by doing business with them or talking at the watercooler and company functions. In doing so, he is bypassing that uncomfortable stage at the beginning of a relationship where he tries to become better acquainted with the woman he is dating and assess whether or not he and she are right for each other. Oftentimes, he can learn a lot about a person with whom he works in a nonthreatening environment and vice versa. Nobody's ego is on the line. Nobody is in the vulnerable position of possibly getting rejected. Another benefit is that two people who work together know the demands of work and the hours that the job demands won't be an issue in a romantic relationship.

A Tricky Situation

As we all know, an office romance can be very tricky. A guy can be getting mixed signals. In other words, he is interacting with a woman and it seems very natural because they are acquaintances from work. He can often make the jump that she is interested in him as more than just a work colleague. He thinks to himself, we seem to get along well, she is attractive, and we already know a lot about each other. Then comes the moment of truth. Will a guy throw caution to the wind and make the next move with this woman? If he can take advantage of this opportunity, maybe he can wind up with a girlfriend or someone to be intimate with, without much effort or risk of getting shot down.

However, other risks are much greater in the work environment. This may cause a guy to hold back. For a man with aspirations of success, the risk of getting caught doing something unprofessional in the workplace can far outweigh the benefits of getting involved in an office romance. The opportunity is always there. It's not as if the man attracted to someone at the office has a random meeting with a woman who's his type, and if he doesn't act immediately he may never see her again. It's convenient because he knows neither he nor the woman is going anywhere, at least not in the short term. She'll be in the office again tomorrow. There's no reason to rush the next move or take unnecessary risks. In the back of his mind the professional man knows that he has all the time in the world. We think that most men would take this longer-term approach with a woman who they believe may have "wife potential." They will most likely get to know a woman like this by working with her and taking the time to allow their friendship to grow first before testing out the dating waters.

We say this because a man who moves quickly on a woman with whom he works may be out for the wrong thing—as far as the woman is concerned. He may be trying to cash in on the mutual attraction and get her into the sack quickly. He feels as though all of the groundwork has been laid by the nature of their interaction together at work. So, beware of a male work colleague who appears to be trying to capitalize on such an easy hit situation. His intentions may not be honorable, and you may wind up in a quick relationship that will inevitably end up being quite messy.

Be sure to let the moment of first attraction pass and give the beginning stages of a relationship time, especially at work. There's no rush. It's a dangerous situation—much better to proceed with caution than to jump too quickly. The opportunity will continue to be there as long as you work together. If neither of you will be leaving any time soon you can seize the opportunity to take the relationship to a personal level anytime. There's no need to push the situation—just allow your connection to grow slowly and naturally if that is what it is meant to do. If a coworker shows a lot of interest right off the bat and then his attention lags, he probably is not looking for a long-term relationship with you. Let him go on to his next sexual conquest.

What Women Can Do

What can you do if you find yourself attracted to a coworker? We suggest you proceed very, very carefully and actually turn down offers to date a coworker just because of the multitude of issues that are involved with dating someone from work. It's best to tell the man who approaches you for a date that you would love to go out, but you are concerned about the risks associated with dating someone at work. Make your concerns clear to him. If, after you've turned him down and time passes, he is still interested, then maybe he could be Mr. Right and venturing out on a date may be worth it for you both. If three months go by and you are still interested in the guy, take him up on his offer to go out. Chances are, if he sticks around this long his interest is in you as a person and not a conquest.

If you do wind up dating a guy from work, we strongly recommend taking each step in the relationship very slowly.

This is especially our advice when it comes to sex. We think you should wait longer than usual—three to four months—before consummating your relationship. Again—wait a while and communicate to him why you want to take it slow. If there's strong chemistry and things are going well, your relationship will only get better and be more intense if you are able to wait and get to know each other better before becoming physically intimate.

Statistically, we know that most relationships just don't work out for one reason or another. We are not trying to be pessimistic here, just realistic. Breakups are very difficult, especially between two people who have been sleeping together. Most couples who split never have to see each other again. Think about how much more complicated a breakup would be if you had to see that person every day at work. Now multiply that by about a hundred times if you found out the coworker who seduced you last night just wanted sex.

So, to recap, here are guidelines for dating a coworker and making it work:

- Turn down his first requests for a date. In fact, don't accept a date unless he persists and asks you repeatedly, in spite of being turned down, for three months. If he's still asking and you are still interested, take him up on the offer.

- Once you do start dating, keep your progress toward intimacy slow and gradual. Don't get too close or too open too fast. This will help you avoid many awkward situations and feelings if things don't work out. (Which is the case in most relationships.) For the first two months, keep dating limited to one time per week. Then two times per week for the next two months, etc.

- Postpone sex even longer than usual; we suggest you hold him off for three to four months.

- As long as you are working together and developing a relationship, be very cautious—for his sake and yours.

5

—

TROUBLESHOOTING COMMITMENT OBSTACLES: PART II

Rebound, Divorce, Children, and Religion

Now we move on to some heavier dating topics. In this look at commitment obstacles, we address the fact that you may be on the rebound, divorced, have children, or practice a different religion than the professional man in whom you are interested. In your letters and e-mails, many of you have asked us about these issues, so you know that they can be speed bumps on or detours off the road to marriage. Based on our experience and insight, we'll help you assess whether there is hope for a long-term relationship when these issues play a part or if you should cut your losses and bail out now. Some of the honest opinions we share may be tough to handle, but as a woman who wants to be thought of as "marriage material," rather than "one-night-stand material," we know you need to hear the answers. Here they are.

On the Rebound

There's no better way to get over your last lover than with the next lover. At least that's what they say. All three of us have had experience dating just after we've been in a serious relationship, and we've dated women who were on the rebound. We know it's a rough time. Used to the comfortable companionship and regular sex of a committed relationship, the person on the rebound is often vulnerable and yearning for these reliable staples as he or she plunges into unpredictable dating waters once again. Given this treacherous combination, rebounders are often known to make the mistake of "settling" on the closest warm body and trying to make a new relationship feel like an established one. As we all know, this rarely works. Whether you are the one who has just come out of a long-term relationship or it's the man you are dating, there are steps you can take to protect yourself as you set out once again in search of happiness and a long-term love.

When You're on the Rebound

We all agree that women who've just come out of a serious relationship carry a tremendous amount of baggage. Ambitious men who have all kinds of tedious and tiresome issues to deal with as they compete in the professional world don't need or want another headache in their lives. So, if they know a woman is on the rebound, they won't target her for an easy, "good for now" girl.

A man may decide to pursue a woman on the rebound if he is attracted to her and thinks she has long-term potential.

As we see it, a woman on the rebound is only worth the effort if she could be a potential wife. The good news is that if a man is dating you and you're coming off a recent breakup, then he must be genuinely interested in you. If the baggage that you bring along doesn't lighten or disappear shortly after he appears, don't expect a man to be around for much longer.

The bad news is that there's only so much a guy can deal with when he knows a woman is mourning the loss of some other man. A guy will test the waters with a woman on the rebound, but he'll do so very cautiously. After all, a man's worst fear is losing a woman he cares about to another man. In the case of a man dating a woman on the rebound, it's as if the old boyfriend or husband is always hanging around, threatening to get back in the picture. Whether or not a rebounder sees or cares about her ex anymore, his presence follows her as long as she talks about the old relationship, seems depressed, or acts pessimistic about men and commitment in general. The thought of a woman he's seriously dating being intimate with another man is difficult for any guy to deal with. When he's seeing a woman coming off a serious relationship, he has to face this thought constantly. You can see why men think twice before dating a woman who's on the rebound.

A man feels even more threatened if he notices the woman grieving over the breakup. Of course, it's natural for her to grieve, and the man should even expect that she would do so. But this will threaten a man's sense of security. Even if a guy intellectually understands what a woman is going through at this point, he will automatically translate her feelings of pain into a lack of feeling for him. In fact, he may even blow the situation out of proportion and start thinking that she is plotting to get back together with her ex and leave him heartbroken.

In general, chances are that a woman on the rebound is not capable of making a man happy. It isn't her fault, she is just emotionally unable to give a man the attention and assurance he needs to take a relationship beyond casual dating. This situation is extremely frustrating to a man and can be enough to drive him away.

Beware of Mr. Competitive

Come to think of it, there is one dangerous type of guy who dates women on the rebound. He is a man in the "must win" mode, and there is one very telling sign that can tip you off to his intentions. He will continuously make references to your ex-boyfriend to ensure that you have absolutely no contact with that guy. He will begin to question you about why you are feeling so bad about losing a man who wasn't good enough for you. In the meantime, even though you are no longer with your ex-boyfriend, Mr. Competitive seems obsessed with winning you away from this other guy at almost any cost. Dating a woman on the rebound contributes to a man's professional, competitive streak, a "win at all costs" attitude.

Ultimately, a guy who feels this way is really being very selfish. All he cares about is being able to win a woman over and feel good about himself. He doesn't really care about who that woman is personally. To him she is a prize. Once she is won, she can be added to his imaginary shelf of trophies, and he can move on to the next. These are the guys you must watch out for. They are extremely insecure men who take advantage of vulnerable women just to make themselves feel better.

Will a Man Commit to a Woman on the Rebound?

The answer is yes. But first she must convince him that whatever she is going through and whatever she is feeling is only natural. A woman must make a man understand that when she is feeling down or lonely or even upset because of a poor past relationship, it has nothing to do with her current situation. Once a man doesn't feel threatened by not making a woman feel good right away, or by the potential of her going back to her ex, then he can settle in and act confidently in the relationship. However, this may be very difficult for a man who has recently been harshly rejected by a woman. What we are saying is that if a man isn't gun shy about being burned, he may give the rebound thing a chance.

Rest assured that a man won't wait for your full attention forever. A man wants to feel as though he makes his girlfriend happy and wants to be the focus of her personal life. If a move toward these states is blocked by a woman's neverending feelings, emotions, and actions regarding her ex-boyfriend, then the relationship is destined for problems in the future.

What Can a Woman Do?

On the rebound and want to increase your chances of landing a man? The most important things you can do to are cut all ties with your ex and be straightforward about your emotional status with the new man in your life.

If you are serious about making this new relationship work, don't see, talk to, or in any way communicate with your ex. Not even in your sleep. Cut all ties to him and any opportunities of getting back together. You must make a strong statement in this regard to prove to your boyfriend that you are truly interested in him, despite all that you've been through with your former man.

Talk to your new guy about how you are feeling. While he may not want to hear that you are still mourning a past relationship, telling him how you feel is better than being silent and letting his imagination run wild. A guy will respect your honesty in this situation. If you allow your new boyfriend to observe your grieving behavior while refusing to explain it, you will only frustrate him and increase the stress that your rebound status puts on your relationship. Despite what people think, men would rather hear the truth and talk about it in this case than put themselves through the torture of thinking their girlfriends are going to leave them. Remember, men are insecure, jealous, and inquisitive. The more details you can give him about how you are feeling while reassuring him of your growing attraction to him, the better off your new guy will be. If you keep this up until your feelings for the old relationship disappear, your man will no longer conjure up the scenario that you are going to leave him or that you aren't attracted to him.

The guys who stay around through all of the trying times do so because they feel a deep connection to a woman that is sustained with open and honest communication. These are the kinds of men you want in your life—the ones who will actually be there through thick and thin.

How to Tip the Odds of Success in Your Favor

- Have no contact with your ex, if possible. Reassure your new man often that things are completely over with your ex-boyfriend and that you have no intention of ever returning to him. Do all you can to put the old relationship out of your mind and focus on the one in which you are involved now.

•   Minimize your new boyfriend's paranoia by reminding him that you are interested in dating him and getting to know him better. Back this up by being available when he asks you out. Respond to his calls quickly. When you are with him, be attentive to him. Show with all your actions that you are there for him.

•   Be patient and understand why your man is acting cautiously. Don't pressure him to move your relationship along more quickly than he wants to. You both need time to get to know each other and have your past relationship fade into a distant memory.

When He's on the Rebound

A man on the rebound is looking to fill the void created by his last breakup. A long-term relationship that ends in heartbreak leaves a gaping hole in a man's heart and life. Feelings of loneliness, insecurity, and failure set in for a man on the rebound, much the same as they do for a woman. Even if he just closed a million-dollar deal, got a great promotion, or his team won the softball league championship, he will feel like less of a man if he has lost the woman he loves. A man in this situation immediately feels he must boost himself up to his accustomed state of confidence. He needs to surround himself with women who will find him attractive, funny, charming, and successful so he can feel good about himself again.

Different men find different kinds of women to fill this role when their hearts are broken. Very, very few men are open to Ms. Right immediately. Most guys can't risk a big rejection again so soon, so they spend a lot of time with friends or "good for now" girls as their broken hearts mend. If you feel seriously about Mr. Rebound, be his friend and be patient. Here's why.

After a long-term relationship ends, both the man and the woman have lost their best friend. Sure men and women are very close to their friends, but they never seem to have that special bond that is shared with their significant others or their lovers. A man can tell his girlfriend things he wouldn't dare tell his friends. Some men would probably rather be caught naked in the middle of a crowded street than have their friends find out some of the thoughts and feelings they've shared with their girlfriends. Once such a relationship is over, a man feels the need to find another best friend.

If you want to get closer to a man on the rebound and don't mind investing some time in him, you can work your way into his life by being his new best friend. This is not a surefire path to becoming his Ms. Right, but being supportive in this time of need could open the door for you. If you want to take this route, don't worry about the relationship progressing or about commitment right away. Just be there when he needs someone to listen to him when he is down or offer company when he is feeling lonely. One day, after this guy has had a chance to lick his wounds and sow his oats, he'll look up and see you there—the woman who knew him through it all.

If you want a chance with Mr. Rebound, you'll probably also have to tolerate hearing about his sexual insecurities. After a breakup, the heartache and feeling of loss sets in, the need for a friend sets in, and a man's desire to talk about and have sex surfaces. You would think that after a breakup, men would be feeling free and excited about the opportunity to meet and have sex with new and different women. It just isn't so. After a breakup a man feels as if every woman in the world is either taken or wouldn't be interested in him anyway. It's a terrible feeling and, on a very frank note, masturbation becomes a very key part of daily life . . . again.

A man on the rebound needs to know that he is sexually desirable. A compliment here and there from you, a woman friend, can do wonders for his sexually distraught ego. You can get a little hint in that you have thought of him as more than a friend and make him feel good by telling him he has a nice body, a butt many women would appreciate, or beautiful eyes. Regular reinforcement of a man's bruised ego can really make him feel more secure during this very insecure time.

You also can't get upset if he wants a whole lot of other women around—the "good for now" crowd. If there was ever a guy who could win a medal for craving sex—and you know how all men want sex—we would say that it would be a guy on the rebound. Of course, a lot of sex always helps those fears of never having sex again to dissipate. Once Mr. Rebound sees that he is sexually desirable, he will not let this opportunity to experience a good batch of women pass him by. Rebounding guys want to chase women again, flirt, get phone numbers, be attractive to women—and of course—have more sex.

When a man is involved in a long-term relationship, many thoughts enter his mind about committing to, getting serious with, moving in with, getting engaged to, and even getting married to one woman. Honestly, a large part of that thought process involves coming to grips with not meeting, dating, or sleeping with any more women. Not now, not ever! Once a man who was in a serious relationship finds himself single again, right away he looks at the bright side. He now has his freedom, and all of his fears of never being with another woman again in his life disappear as his little black book fills up with fresh names and numbers.

When it comes to their hearts and women they sense might be able to win them, men on the rebound are extremely cautious. Men who get hurt in relationships are very hard on themselves emotionally. They tend to look at themselves as losers and wonder why they are crying or why they are feeling so down about a relationship that is over. They may mistakenly feel that their macho guy friends would never be crying like a baby or feeling so torn up inside if faced with the same situation. Quite often a man starts to question himself as a man because he is feeling so hurt and so down about the loss of his girlfriend. Men aren't supposed to cry, and men aren't supposed to be hurt by women. So when it does happen, a man is very cautious about putting himself in a situation where it can happen to him again. Yes, this might even mean that Mr. Rebound will forgo getting into a serious relationship for a long time just to avoid the possibility of another breakup and the terrible pain that can accompany it. In a very rare case, Mr. Rebound will open himself up to Ms. Right at this point, but nine out of ten guys will take this time to get back on their feet.

Will a Man on the Rebound Commit?

As a general rule, we must say no, not right away. Not to say that there aren't exceptions, but usually there's just too much going on for him to focus on committing—even to a woman who he thinks of as "marriage material"—immediately. There is hope, though. If a woman is willing to be patient, she can often work things out with Mr. Rebound in the long run.

What Can a Woman Do?

If you choose to get involved with a man on the rebound, be sure to take things slowly and cautiously. He may act like Prince Charming in an effort to win you over. This is usually quite easy for him to do since he is used to being nice and caring in his previous long-term relationship. He can then just carry this over into his new relationship with you. However, if he hasn't taken the proper time to heal and reflect on his past relationship, let alone get to know you, problems and further heartache lie ahead.

When you are dating, beware of men on the rebound. They may wine and dine you and drive you wild with their charm, but there is a lot going through their minds, the last of which is getting serious with you. As we have pointed out, you should avoid getting into the girlfriend mode with this rebound man. Since we know how susceptible women are to men in romance overdrive, we're going to say it again—it's easy for a guy to be in the "boyfriend" mode if he is coming off a relationship, because he is used to that mode. If you succumb to his romantic advances before he's ready to open up and become truly intimate, you'll have blown your chances with him. We have seen so many cases in which a woman mistook a man's intentions because he appeared to be so into the relationship, when in fact he was just picking up where he left off with his ex-girlfriend. Take things slowly. Be the friend that Mr. Rebound needs at the beginning.

In case you aren't picking up on our message, let us be very clear here. We think it is extremely important in "rebound" circumstances that you don't have sex with this guy early on. This is a surefire way of getting put on his perennial "good for now" girl list. This might be tricky because having sex is exactly what a guy wants at this critical time. But be strong. Once you have sex, Mr. Rebound most likely won't take the time to get to know you. In fact, he will be looking for the next woman to get into the sack with.

The more cautious you are in these situations, the better chances you have of a longer-lasting relationship. Remember, this guy is looking to find that lost comfort zone with a woman. He probably isn't looking to get serious, and he is probably extremely afraid of getting hurt again. The more restrained you can be, the better chance you have of really getting to know each other well. Start out as friends, not lovers. It is the companionship that a man needs now, whether he knows it or not. If he is getting it, he'll see you whether you are having sex or not. The longer you spend time together, the more his broken heart will mend and the more attached to you he will become. The more attached you become, the better the odds are of your actually falling in love with each other.

Oh and one more thing, don't try to play "shrink" with the guy. The last thing he wants to do is talk about his ex. You may want to know exactly how the breakup happened and why, but he is not going to want to talk about it. He may be in too much pain or still uncertain about what he wants to do—go back to her, stay with you, or play the field. We three agree that you shouldn't push this topic of conversation. Though you may think you are missing out on a very insightful piece of information, you are not. Whether he dumped her or she dumped him is of little consequence. A guy on the rebound may decide to go back to his ex either way.

There are no guarantees, and dating a man on the rebound

is risky business. However, there is a possibility of landing a great guy if you play your cards right. If you think that this guy could be "the one" for you, you shouldn't pass him by just because he is on the rebound. All it means is that you have to understand what he is thinking, and what he wants from you. Take it slow, let your relationship develop naturally, and he's yours.

Chris's friend Marsha, a smart and pretty thirty-year-old who was working her way up in a successful catering business, found her Mr. Right when his previous girlfriend of four years, Tammy, had just broken up with him. Marsha met Danny, a thirty-two-year-old chief financial officer for a cosmetics company, at a good friend's party. For years, Marsha had heard the party's hostess, Andrea, talk about what a nice guy Danny was. When Marsha met him and talked to him at the party, she had to agree. Marsha knew she was interested in Danny romantically, but realized he probably wasn't over the breakup yet. She took it slow and concentrated on being his friend first. She suggested they go in-line skating in Central Park, a passion she learned they shared from their conversation. Danny took Marsha up on her offer and they had a great time the next afternoon.

Though Marsha found Danny very cute—she loved his red hair and boyish smile—she kept her flirting to a bare minimum in the first months they got to know each other. She pretended not to hear any of the suggestive innuendoes that Danny slid into the conversation early on. She and Danny went hiking and running together. One Saturday, Marsha surprised Danny with a trip to an amusement park. They met at sports bars to watch Yankee games and their evenings ended with a friendly wave or hug. Sometimes they'd meet up with friends on these evenings, so she got to know his crowd and he got to know hers. They did things in groups and they did things alone together, but none of what Marsha and Danny shared had the feel of a date. Danny sometimes told Marsha about his dates, none of which seemed to be growing into serious relationships. Of course, it wasn't easy for Marsha to hear about the other women in Danny's life, but she was wise enough to know that those were strictly "good for now" girls. Marsha was confident enough to take her time with Danny. She wanted him for the long term. Marsha was smart to become Danny's pal first.

They had known each other six months when Marsha asked Danny if he'd like to watch a football game at her place. She offered to cook dinner. He loved the idea. They ate the burgers she made and drank the beer he brought while the game went into overtime. When the news came on, Danny and Marsha realized they had been sitting very close on the couch and were holding hands. Danny turned and gave Marsha a kiss and she kissed him back. Marsha took this opportunity to tell Danny that she did think of him as more than a friend and hoped maybe he felt the same way about her. Danny said he liked the way Marsha had been able to lift his spirits in the time following his breakup with Tammy. Marsha escorted Danny to the door and gave him a lingering good night kiss and said she hoped they could see each other again soon.

Danny went home that evening thinking a lot about Marsha. He called her the next day and asked her out for a Saturday night date the following week. He took her to dinner at a restaurant and they went out dancing afterward at a club. That was the first of many dates that Marsha and Danny went on in the months to follow. They got closer and more intimate slowly and Danny told Marsha he realized that his previous relationship had not fulfilled him the way this one did. He told Marsha he felt comfortable with her in almost any situation and that he'd always felt a little off balance with Tammy, even when times were good. Marsha was thrilled to hear this because it was exactly how she felt about Danny. She knew that her patience and slow approach with him had paid off. She moved in with Danny eight months after that first great date.

One Sunday Tammy turned up at their door, and without a moment of hesitation, Danny invited her in and introduced her to his new girlfriend, Marsha. Tammy said she just wanted to see how Danny was doing, commented that he looked very happy, and left soon after. Marsha suspected that Tammy had really stopped by to see if she could get back with Danny, but was sure there was no chance of that. Marsha was very impressed by how confidently Danny had handled Tammy's visit. Marsha trusted Danny and felt their relationship was strong enough to last a lifetime. Danny came to feel the same way. On a trip to Ireland two years later, he proposed.

Positive signs to look for in the man on the rebound:

- He has come to grips with the breakup. He seems more confident and easygoing.

- He begins to open up to you more and is treating you like his best friend. He confides in you, and you spend a good deal of time talking on the phone with him and hanging out together.

- A slow road to sex. Men on the rebound need sex. If he isn't pushing the issue with you, this is a good sign that he isn't keeping you around solely with the hope that you'll sleep with him.

Some negative signs:

- He continues to tell you he doesn't want to get involved in a serious relationship. He wants to date many women and sow more oats.

- He shows a lack of self-respect by talking about how he still feels responsible for the breakup. He says he views himself as a failure because the relationship didn't work out. He is depressed and unmotivated. This is a man who is a long way from being able to settle into new commitment with you.

- He keeps harping on how he feels gun shy, or he acts that way. Even if he is feeling good about himself and is over the breakup, he may still be apprehensive about opening up and getting close to you for fear of being hurt again. He doesn't confide in you, and you still feel as if he is a stranger although you've been seeing him as a friend for months.

The Divorced Woman

Divorced women are by far the largest group of women who have contacted us since *What Men Want* was published. We never realized how tough it must be for someone who has been married to be thrown back into the dating scene again. The most popular question we receive is "How do guys feel about dating divorced women?" Divorced women want to know when they should tell a man that they've been married before, if at all. This group of women also wanted to know how and where to meet single professional men, since they have been out of the dating scene for so long. Fortunately, we've had experience dating divorced

women, and we are here to tell you how men like us feel
about it.

What Is He Thinking?

Basically, the single professional man who has never been
married is quite cautious about dating divorced women. The
first thought guys like us usually have about a woman who
tells us she is divorced is that if she was divorced once, she
could divorce again. A man's irrational fear of being a future
divorce victim gets to him before he can even think about
the individual woman in question.

Obviously, divorce is not something anyone plans for, but
it is dreaded by every guy. As crazy or unfair as it may be,
knowing that a particular woman has experienced this horri-
fying break in married life—a condition he would like to
think will last forever for him and Ms. Right—a man considers immediately the chance that she is predisposed to divorce.
You may be thinking that this line of thought sounds a bit
hysterical. Consider for a moment that divorce is, perhaps,
the greatest symbol of rejection for a single professional man.

Men fear that being a boyfriend or a second husband will
mean playing second fiddle to the first guy a woman married. He fears the divorced woman will always be comparing
him to her ex-husband and that her family and friends won't
take his relationship now or a wedding in the future with her
seriously.

In addition, when a man is dating a woman who's been
divorced, he is constantly wondering how she could ever
truly fall in love with him and know that it will be forever.
Obviously she felt this way once before and it didn't work
out. She was so in love with her ex-husband when they got
married; surely she thought it would be a lifelong union. But

they wound up getting divorced. Immediately a single, professional guy wonders how a divorcée could fall in love with him—and remain in love with him, forever. His ego will always be sensitive as he worries if he will go the way of the first guy.

A man who has never been married before feels as though he will never escape the fact that a divorced woman was once in love and committed to someone else. He imagines that no matter how long it has been since she and the other guy parted, there will always be something that comes up as a reminder of her previous union with him. This new man in her life knows he may come across old bank accounts, telephone bills, changes of address, a driver's license, health insurance forms, or other pieces of her past that will remind him that she was once Mrs. So and So before she met him. All of the thoughts of his uneasiness about dating a divorced woman he had when he first met her will flood back, or so he thinks, when he envisions commitment to the woman who once was married to someone else. A guy will feel frustrated and begin to wonder why he didn't meet someone like himself, someone who had never been married before. If that were the case, he would never have to deal with any of these issues that bring to mind previous husband(s) and make him so uncomfortable.

All of these problems arise because this new guy knows that at one time another man was the center of this woman's life—the woman he loves. He wants to be the center of her life now and always. The thought that he's stepping into a role that has been played by some other man makes him feel as though he is competing with or being compared to someone else and that this feeling will last as long as this relationship does. At these times, a man is forced to see his girlfriend as the wife of another man. That is hard for him to swallow.

It can be very uncomfortable for the man if the woman he is seeing has issues she needs to go over with her ex-husband. A single professional man will become more and more frustrated each time he's reminded of this other guy. It often takes a very long time for all of the past really to be in the past and for a woman never to have the need to deal with her previous husband(s). This may be too long a period for some men to wait around.

These issues are heightened if a woman maintains any regular contact with her ex-husband, which, from what we've seen, is quite common. The new boyfriend or husband will be jealous, insecure, worried that a woman's ex-husband might upset her or want her back . . . these are just a few of the things that run through a man's head when thinking about his girlfriend dealing with her ex-husband. Believe us, none of these thoughts are very pleasant. A man feels incredibly helpless in these situations. There's just nothing he can do to intervene without making this issue an even larger one. To further complicate an already complicated situation, most divorces are not amicable. Mutual resentment may keep flaring up, which may push a man dating a divorced woman even farther away.

Sometimes either an ex-husband wants his ex-wife back or vice versa. When a man wants the woman back and she is dating someone else, this can turn the new guy's life into a total nightmare.

Rich has a friend, John, a never-been-married, thirty-year-old stockbroker, who started dating Nancy, a twenty-nine-year-old computer consultant who was recently divorced. Initially, John was hesitant to get involved with Nancy, but he hit it off with her on their first date and soon the fact that she was divorced slipped into the back of his mind. They had been dating for about a year when they went out to dinner and John noticed Nancy seemed distant and nervous. When John asked what was wrong, Nancy explained that Luke, her ex, had been calling her and stopping by. He wanted to get back together. She assured John that she had no desire to rekindle her relationship with Luke.

John believed Nancy but felt very insecure. Here he was, dating a woman who has another man calling her all the time. Not just some strange man, but a man whom she once loved and shared her life with. John tried to feel confident but he knew Luke and Nancy had a history together and that would give Luke leverage over him. Despite what Nancy said about how solid she and John were, John felt he couldn't compete with the previous Mr. Right. He sensed that Nancy could say with no notice, "I'm going to give it a try one more time with Luke. I mean we did share a life together and maybe we deserve to try to make it work again." He envisioned her saying something like, "I really can't handle this relationship we are in. I'm confused about getting divorced, I really need to think things out and this relationship is just too much for me at this point in my life."

John was tortured. No man would be able to stay in a relationship in which he thinks this talk is going to come up and remain sane. Though he cared for Nancy, John ended up leaving the relationship two months after Luke returned to the scene. He just couldn't stand the thought of falling more deeply in love with Nancy only to have Luke win her back.

In the end, every man wants to see himself as the one and only man for his girlfriend, fiancée, or wife. Any references or incidents that get in the way of this vision can put a man on guard and send him away from the path to commitment.

Will He Commit?

We've just shared a pretty bleak picture that single professional men conjure up when they consider dating a woman who was once married to someone else, but there is some good news. Although the odds may seem against it, we believe that men like us (who are young, single and have never been married) can fall in love with divorced women and marry them. So there's hope for all of you divorcées out there, but you must be cognizant of the possible snags we mentioned above.

Our friend, Allan, a successful investment banker at thirty-three, never thought he'd marry a divorced woman, but that didn't stop him when he fell in love with one. He had always wanted the perfect love story: single boy, never married, meets single girl, never married, they fall in love, get married, and live happily ever after. Most of the time Allan was so busy with work that he didn't have to worry about any women—divorced or otherwise. Then, Cupid's arrow hit him when he least expected it. Allan was on a plane to Nebraska for business and a woman sat down next to him. Busy reading his notes for work, Allan didn't pay any attention to his seatmate until a stewardess walking by accidentally spilled a drink on her. Allan offered to help out and made light of the embarrassing situation. The woman, Leslie, and he began talking. Allan found out that Leslie worked in insurance and was also traveling from New York to do business in Nebraska. Leslie and Allan chatted for the whole plane ride and made plans to have dinner together when they landed. Over dinner Leslie told Allan she had been divorced for two years and her ex-husband had moved to L.A. Allan found this woman so interesting and exciting he dismissed his rule about not getting serious with divorcées. He knew he wanted to get to know Leslie better. They saw each other when they got back to New York and a year and a half later Allan proposed and Leslie accepted.

A multitude of fears may make a man hesitate and in some cases even back away from a relationship with you if you are divorced, but he can also commit to you and fall in love if you know his fears and take the right steps to allay them. You should avoid the references to your previous husband that make him uncomfortable and insecure. You must also do all you can to put the new Mr. Right at ease. Your boyfriend must feel comfortable not only about your relationship with him but about your relationship with your ex-husband as well. He must fully understand that your previous marriage is completely over . . . a thing of the past. You must limit your contact with your ex-husband, eventually moving toward no contact at all, if possible. Of course, if you and your ex are parents, you will continue to meet regarding the children. We will discuss how to handle this later in the chapter.

Age may play a part in such a situation as well. For example, when a younger, single, never-been-married man meets a divorced woman of any age, he may feel uncomfortable dating her. If a man is older than a previously married woman, it might be somewhat easier for him to adjust to her divorced status. Maybe older men have had enough experience with relationships to know when a woman says "the marriage is over," it really is over. Or, perhaps older men are just more willing to take a risk with a younger woman no matter what her marital status may be. An older man may also be single after having been in a marriage or two himself and understand that love can come again, and may even be better when a woman has been married and experienced all it has to offer—good and bad.

Making the Way for Commitment

There are plenty of things you can do if you are a divorced woman looking for commitment from a single professional man. First, keep things fresh. Everything you do in your relationship with a man who has never been married has to be completely new and exciting. You must do things that you haven't done in the past so your life together is full of new experiences for both of you. For example, if you used to go camping with your ex-husband, don't pack up the same equipment and return to the same places with your new boyfriend. Not only would this probably be strange for you, but it will lack the excitement of a fresh experience. You should share the thrill of adventure together. Travel to new places, search for a new apartment together, and try new restaurants. Take up new activities and spend time on them with your boyfriend. Have both of you wanted to snorkel or in-line skate, paint or horseback ride, play golf or go hiking but never had the chance to before? Now is the time to explore these new things with him. Sharing brand-new experiences and learning skills with your boyfriend will keep things exciting and healthy for both of you and help ensure the success of your relationship.

Second, you better have a very good excuse for the divorce. Don't fabricate a story, but very clearly outline the problems that brought your last marriage down. For example, don't say that a marriage didn't work out because you were too young when you got married and leave it at that. This just won't cut it. A man will think that you don't know any better now than you did when you first walked down the aisle. If you left your ex-husband because he was mentally or physically abusive to you or cheated on you, then it is understood that the divorce happened for a valid and completely understandable reason.

When your new man asks you about what happened with the last marriage, as he surely will, be prepared. Take this one opportunity to talk about the specific issues that came between you and your ex and drove you apart. Clearly outline the steps you have taken since then—whether they be therapy or a long period away from the dating scene—so that the next relationship you have will last. This will help ease the fears of the man you are dating. As you now know, you will be addressing some of the thoughts that are going through his mind—whether he shares them with you or not.

The most important move you can make in your new relationship is to get all of the logistics of your divorce behind you before you become closely involved with another man. Don't let your new guy find a check from your ex-husband to reimburse you for half of the old phone bill. Don't let him hear a message from your ex-husband on your answering machine about meeting to sign some legal papers. Get all that stuff completely out of your life before you date someone new. If that is not possible for whatever reason, don't let your new man know that you are cleaning up some final details with the ex. You never know, these little details can be the difference between keeping a man around forever and having him jump ship before it takes on too much water.

We hope that our being frank with you about how the single professional man feels about dating divorced women doesn't discourage you. Knowing what a man is thinking and fearing about entering into a relationship with you will help you become more confident when you do date. Now you know where the land mines are and how to step around them if you are working toward a successful long-term relationship with the single, professional Mr. Right. Let's revisit the important points one more time.

Our Tips on Landing a Single Professional Man if You Are Divorced

• Spin the negatives of your old relationship into positives. You now have the experience to know what didn't work in your previous relationship, and you won't make the same mistakes again. Whenever possible, use your experiences to your advantage. A man appreciates a woman who knows herself and can cut through the silly relationship games. Show your openness and maturity.

• Live this relationship as if it were your first. Show your excitement about becoming committed, getting engaged, and planning the wedding as if you'd never done it before. This will avoid making your new man feel as if he lost out on the thrill of getting married by choosing to settle down with a divorced woman.

• Make your new man feel as though he is the only man in your life now. Help him imagine that he has always been number one—do this by keeping references to previous marriages nonexistent or very rare. Now and in the future, do whatever you can to keep your contact with your ex—via telephone and in person—to a bare minimum and, if possible, avoid it completely.

• Reassure your man that your life with your ex is completely over. Do all you can to show that it is your new man whom you love. Write him love letters, call him to say that you are thinking of him, and spend special dinners and weekends away completely focused on him. If you do, you will help keep his thoughts about you having had a life with someone before him at bay. He will feel more comfortable about becoming close and open with you and will move the relationship to the next level.

When You Are Not Alone:
The Woman with Children

Women with children represent another large group from whom we receive many letters and e-mails. These women want to know what guys like us think about dating single mothers. To be honest, knowing a woman has one or more children does make us think twice before asking her out. There are just so many difficult things a man has to consider when dating a woman with a child. They can be high hurdles to the success of any long-term relationship.

Keep in mind that the three of us do not have any children and this is the perspective you are getting. We would imagine that divorced men who have children would be much more comfortable dating women who are single moms. Older men who have never had children may also welcome a ready-made family. These might be very important factors for you to keep in mind as you look for Mr. Right.

In fact, we asked the single men in their forties and fifties with whom we work what their opinions were when it came to dating women with children. They gave us feedback that was very different from our reactions. They didn't mind dating women with children at all. Many of them welcomed it. They liked the grounded and mature qualities women who are mothers have. Some of these guys were divorced fathers whose ex-wives had custody of the kids and they told us they missed having children around all the time and would welcome a relationship that came with children. Fathers or not, most of the men we spoke to said if Ms. Right were a mom already they would be happy to help her raise the children if they were younger, or just get to know them if they were older. These men understood that children might complicate the picture but they focused on the positive aspects of parenthood.

From our perspective, finding, meeting, and having a long-lasting relationship with a woman is difficult enough without having a child in the picture. As we've told you, men are basically insecure when it comes to dating. The thought that rejection may come at any point in a relationship is difficult for us to deal with. We like to keep our exposure to the pain of such a situation as low as possible. To us it seems children add just one more big reason why things might not work out with a woman. This isn't to say that we would never consider a woman with a child to be "marriage material." Ms. Right may just have a child or two. As we've said many times before, Ms. Right can come along at any time and surprise us. From a general perspective, dating single mothers just isn't something we'd rush toward.

First, in this case, a man has to think about the importance of not only being accepted by a woman but by her children as well. The possibility and fear of rejection can be very high from a man's point of view. After all, women may be a mystery to us, but children usually are a foreign country entirely to young single men. To think that a little child could be the source of his rejection puts a man on very uncertain and perhaps very defensive ground. Many men don't want to put themselves in such a vulnerable position.

When a man dates a woman with a child, he immediately feels that he not only must win the woman over but that he must win the child over as well. It's difficult enough for a man and a woman to fall in love and get through all of the obstacles that present themselves as a relationship becomes intimate. Having a child in the picture simply adds another hurdle. A man wonders, "What if the child doesn't like me? What if I don't like the child?" These issues can cause serious strains on relationships. The fear of all of this up front may, in fact, be enough to make a man turn away from a relationship with a single mother before it starts just to avoid having to deal with such dangers.

Then there is the issue of the time and responsibility a child requires from parents. As we highlight time and again in these pages, professional men are very serious about their careers. Entering into a relationship with a woman who has a child, a single professional man immediately thinks of the added obligation of parenthood. He thinks about where he is in his career and where he wants to go. It seems there are not enough hours in a day for him to achieve his goals. He is overwhelmed by the thought of trying to launch a successful relationship and then become an instant dad if things work out. "I just don't have the time or energy for this," he concludes before he even asks a woman out on a first date.

A man also has fears about the ex-husband or boyfriend, the child's father, always being in the picture. As we said in the section about dating divorced women, it's terrible having a woman's ex-lover in the picture constantly. If the father has any sort of relationship with the child, this scenario is unavoidable. Let's face it. The ex will be around forever. No matter how distant the girlfriend's ex may be, the new guy will have an everlasting reminder that she was in love with— and made love to—another man. As we've discussed earlier, a very vivid picture gets painted in a man's mind when he thinks about his girlfriend, fiancée, or wife, having sex with another man, no matter how far in the past it occurred. Given this, having a built-in ex for life is not a very attractive proposition for any man to consider.

Even worse is having the child around every day to be a constant reminder of his girlfriend's ex. Imagine what a man thinks about. Another man's sperm fertilized her egg and created this child. This is torture for a man to deal with. He will paint the most vivid picture in his mind about his wife and her ex-husband and their child. The reason why a man will do this is that he will constantly be considering the fact that there are other women out there without the baggage of an ex and a child. He will often consider getting out of a relationship with a single mother to find another woman without baggage.

In addition, a man will feel that he will never be liked or respected by the child's father. You may think, "So what?" But this is a big guy thing. No man can like another man who is sleeping with his ex. No man can like another man who used to sleep with his wife. No man can possibly like another man raising his child. It's a male territorial issue, plain and simple. Since every man has strong primal feelings in this regard, the boyfriend of a single mom will know that he will never have a comfortable relationship with the father of the child. So, he adds another unnecessary strain to a list of growing strains with which he'll have to live if he has a relationship with a woman who has a child.

Considering a relationship with a single mother also may leave a man feeling out of control of his own life. A professional man needs time to plan his future, and a very large consideration in his life is when to have children. Dating a woman with a child immediately takes that decision away from him, gives him no leeway, and forces him into a situation that he hasn't had ample time to consider. This is the exact opposite of how professional men like to live their lives and make major life decisions. When he looks at a woman with children, a single professional man sees the two most important decisions in his life—getting married and having children—now being combined into a single decision. Getting married and becoming an instant stepfather is quite an overwhelming set of circumstances for any man. Not only has he lost his vote as to when children would be a good addition to his life but he faces instant responsibility for a child that is not his own.

A man's first thought will be that he is getting the sloppy seconds of parenthood. Like a divorced woman who has obviously already had one wedding, a woman with a child has already experienced the thrill of the first child—without him. We are here to tell you that having a child and sharing the new experience of raising that child together with his wife is something a man looks forward to. If a woman already has a child, the opportunity to raise a child for the first time together is lost.

On top of all of this, there are financial considerations. If a man is going to get serious with a woman who has a child, in his mind he must automatically become the financial provider for that child. There's no way to avoid that feeling. You can't just have the woman and not the child, and you must then treat the child as if he were your own. That places a large financial burden on a man who may not be ready for it at that stage in his life.

Will a Professional Man Commit to a Woman Who Has a Child?

Although dating a woman with a child is not what we see as the optimal choice for a professional guy who has never been married and has no children, it does happen, and it can turn into a long-lasting relationship that can lead to marriage. So, for all of you single mothers who have written to us and e-mailed us, there's definitely hope that you will land a great man.

We do feel that the odds for your getting married are much better if you date men who already have children, as they will probably have a lot more in common with you, or older men who might love an instant family. Many of the fears and concerns we have described above will not be such big issues for a man who is a father himself, or is mature enough to jump right into parenthood.

How to Spot and Keep the New Mr. Right

If you have your eyes on a young guy who is professional, single, and without children who you think may be your Mr. Right—go for it. Follow our advice as you move into the relationship to soothe any fears he has. If you don't have a particular guy in mind and are just looking to better your chances at building a future long-term relationship, remember what we've said about older men and men who have children—single men, of course. We think a good strategy might also be to consider divorced men as well, even men divorced from a childless marriage. They have already been through marriage and most likely don't have the same concerns other single men may have, such as the worry about becoming an instant father or having to provide for a child who isn't theirs.

Rich knows Murray, a single doctor in his mid-fifties, who turned out to be Mr. Right for a divorced woman with children. Growing up, Murray was raised with three brothers and two sisters. He yearned to have a house filled with the activity and love that only a wife and children bring, but the years went by quickly and Murray focused on building his pediatric practice. Then, at a friend's summer barbecue, Murray met Grace, a forty-something single mom with two children; Sally, eight, and Brendon, ten. Murray laughed at Grace's jokes and witty remarks. Grace loved that Murray played catch with the children for half the afternoon. The two started dating and in six months they were engaged. Three years later, Grace and Murray were the proud parents of a new baby girl, Isabel. Murray says these are the happiest years of his life.

Guys like Murray are the exception. They are out there, but in general, single mothers need to be very cautious of single men. Beware, they may be sweet-talking you and treating you well just for sex. Most single men will automatically put women with children in the "good for now" category. Since these guys are interested only in a short-term companion, younger, never-been-married men have a good chance of causing you heartache and pain.

One telltale sign of a man's interest is his interaction with your child. If he puts off meeting your son or daughter, then chances are he doesn't have any interest in you for the long term. Once you decide to introduce a man to your child, which you should do only after dating him for a few months, you will be able to tell his interest in you by how he interacts with the child. If he is going the extra mile to get to know your child as opposed to just going through the motions, he may just have you in the "marriage material" category. This is the kind of guy you want to hold on to.

To Recap: Moves for Success

• Consider dating older men, divorced men, or men who have children.

• Alleviate your boyfriend's concerns about becoming a parent sooner than he had planned—reassure him that you're not looking for an instant father for your child.

• Reassure your boyfriend that the child's father won't be around for any other reason than to see the child.

• Make him aware that you can provide for the child and that you don't expect him to carry any financial responsibilities for the child.

• Share the rewards of being a parent with your new man by telling him touching or funny stories about your child. Eventually, plan activities you and he and your child can enjoy together—going to the park, the movies, or having lunch together. Add these to the times you and he spend alone; don't let these take the place of your dates.

When You Practice Different Religions

Being of a different religious persuasion can be an issue for some professional men and a non-issue for others. For some men, the fact that you practice a different faith from his can be a "deal breaker." The seriousness of this issue depends on how the man you are dating has been raised and what his family thinks about interreligious marriages.

If a man really cares about marrying a woman of the same religion, and he is dating a woman who practices a different religion, when should he tell her this? If the relationship is just starting out and he is having fun but doesn't see her as a "marriage material" girl then there really is no need to tell her. He will keep quiet. If religion is important to him or he senses that it is a key issue for a woman he believes has "wife potential," a guy will always wonder how and when he should bring this issue up. That doesn't mean he will bring it up right away. Early on, many men will tend to push this and other serious issues aside, not wanting to introduce a problem into a relationship that seems to be going very smoothly. This can be dangerous and will always come back to haunt the couple who procrastinates.

Our experience has also taught us that our parents and the parents of women we have dated can feel very strongly about religion and may put pressure on their children to marry within their faith. They always use their "life experience" as a credential and tell you that no matter how in love you are at the moment, religious issues can tear couples apart in the future. We don't think that parents are right, necessarily, but you should be aware of the added stress that different religious perspectives can put on a relationship.

We have noticed that once a couple decides they would rather be together than apart in spite of different, strongly held religious beliefs, the issue of converting to a partner's religion comes up. The question arises: which one should convert and why? Will the church or temple accept this person even if he wants to convert? If so, will he have to be reeducated? Will he have time to go through the process?

From our experience different faiths are not really the core issue. Often, the major question is how the children will be raised. Should they be raised following the man's religion or the woman's religion? If a choice is made, then how will the other spouse feel once children are born? This decision is one that needs to be made well in advance by two people who have no experience making such decisions. Don't underestimate the seriousness of this question and the problems it could cause in your relationship. Talk about it and be honest about how you feel as soon as you see a relationship is getting serious with a man of a different religion.

As you can see, interfaith romances between two people with strong beliefs can force a couple to deal with major life issues very early in their relationship. We are not discussing this to scare anybody away from dating someone outside of her religion. In fact, we all have done it and we all understand that it's quite possible to fall madly in love with someone of a different religious persuasion. But we also know how terrible it can feel to have to decide between a woman whom you love and religion. After all, a strong relationship full of love doesn't come around too often in a lifetime. It would be a shame to throw it all away because an amicable compromise can't be reached.

What You Can Do

We couldn't begin to have all the answers when it comes to this touchy and controversial topic. We are adamantly against trying to sweep the issue under the rug. Of course, it's easier not to pay attention to the problem and avoid unwanted stress on the relationship. That strategy will simply come back to haunt you in the end.

We encourage you to be honest with yourself first. Think seriously about how you feel toward the religion issue. Don't compromise your true feelings because you are desperate for a husband. Your time for love and companionship with the right man will always come. The worst thing you could do would be to allow yourself to believe that dating someone outside your religion is not a big deal, when deep down in your heart you know that it is.

Second, you have to get a feeling about how your man stands on the issue. Now remember, men don't like to talk about the relationship. Though you must treat this issue with kid gloves, this is one subject you can't allow him to avoid. You must know, and you must know early on, what his views are when it comes to dating someone who practices another religion. If he dodges the issue with you, you must get out of the relationship. His failure to address the topic simply means that it's an important issue to him that in time will cause great strain or the end of your relationship. Think about it: if the subject didn't mean anything to him, it wouldn't be a burden to discuss.

If you have found Mr. Right and he is of a different religious persuasion, you might speak with a clergy member, or some family members (sometimes other than parents), or elders whom you feel you can trust to give you the guidance and advice you may need in a difficult situation like this. If religion is a nonnegotiable issue for you and you are looking for a serious relationship, you may want to consider dating only those of the same faith as yourself to avoid this situation in the future.

Please, please don't underestimate the importance of this issue on a relationship. We have experienced and seen relationships in which the religion issue was glossed over, neglected, and not discussed, and ultimately tore couples apart. Sure there are compromises, like nonsecular or interfaith weddings. There are even ways to raise children and have them educated in both religions until they feel comfortable making their own decision. Compromise is always an option. Avoidance is a surefire way to ensure that a relationship either fizzles or faces serious pressure and strains as the result of the issue not being dealt with openly.

Our Tips for Having a Discussion with a Man on Religion

• Realize the issue cannot be swept under the carpet and make talking about it with your boyfriend a priority.

• Your first attempts at addressing the issue of religion should be informal—an information-gathering session in which both of you simply state your feelings about your religious beliefs and their importance to you. At this point, avoid specific discussions about your future together.

• Discuss the idea of compromise to see if either of you is open to it. Keep it general—don't focus on specifics yet.

• Once you have the preliminary discussions—take some time so you each can process what was said. Try to figure out if there is a possibility of working things out.

• If not—realize that you can't force it. Face that religion will remain a major obstacle, and it will always be there, linger-

ing. Take steps to move the relationship from a romantic interest to one that is for fun, or friendship. If you can't do that,
end it.

• If you can figure out a way to make your relationship
work, great. Be aware that as the relationship continues new
issues may come up, or you may discover that one of you is not
as flexible as you originally thought.

• This is potentially a very sticky situation. Be sure to treat
it very delicately in discussions and respect each other's differences.

• If your parents or his feel strongly that you should not
become an interfaith couple, you and your man must approach
them as a team, having already worked out the details. You cannot please everyone, so focus on what will satisfy you and your
partner and make a strong unified presentation of your position
to your folks. Make it clear to your parents that you have
thought the situation through and know the roles your differ-
ing faiths will play in your lives and the lives of any children you
might have. Don't allow them to think you can be swayed on
any point. If you do, they will surely try to influence you at the
expense of your relationship.

6

—

SEX AND THE
COMMITTED RELATIONSHIP

Hopefully, what we have shared in the previous chapters will help you parlay an early spark and common ground with a professional man into the start of a long-term, committed relationship. If your connection with Mr. Right is to grow strong and lasting, it must be accompanied by a developing intimacy and a physical relationship as you get to know each other better. Yes, we are taking about sex. You may be surprised at what we are about to divulge regarding how men approach monogamy. That's why we thought it important to cover the sexual issues that you will inevitably face as you move from wife potential to wife. You may not have as much to fear as you think when it comes to him being faithful. But sex is also a potential minefield for the girl whom a man classifies as "marriage material" in the beginning of a relationship. In some cases, one wrong word or move can land you in his "good for now" girl column forever. To stay off that list, you'll want to read this chapter carefully, very carefully.

Addressing the Sex-with-One-Woman-Forever Syndrome

Sex and the committed relationship. The juxtaposition of these two thoughts—sex and commitment—strikes at the greatest fear in a man. We have said it before and we will say it again, men have a constant fear of never again having sex with another woman. We love a variety of sexual partners. This keeps sex exciting for us. However, we do know that there comes a time in life when sex with only one woman will have to suffice if we want to have that one special woman, that Ms. Right by our side. Hey, why shouldn't it suffice? We love this woman, she is our best friend, she loves us, and we enjoy one another's company. When we hear the upside of commitment like this, it sounds great. But we'd be lying to you if we said it was easy for us to accept the vision of the single sexual partner for life and make good on our commitment to her.

We know that many of you fear your Mr. Right may be wrestling with the thought of long-term monogamy. We want to help you understand that just because your guy may feel this way about sex and commitment, he won't necessarily be unfaithful to you. He understands the damage infidelity can do to a long-term relationship and, frankly, he can't afford such fallout if he is an ambitious man with high professional goals for his future. A professional man wants his life to unfold as he plans it—a happy committed relationship that eventually involves getting married and having children is usually part of his vision. A professional man takes certain steps to diminish the constant temptation of sex with others as a committed man. We'll tell you about these. We will also share what you can do to keep that sexual spark with your man fresh, man's most popular fantasy, the insecurities that can derail commitment (for him and you), and what you should never tell your man about your sex life if you want his commitment to last.

How to Keep Him Excited, Curious, and Satisfied

No couple could keep the kind of passion they had in the first round of sex together through a whole lifelong relationship. In a committed relationship, we all know that usually we don't have wild and crazy sex every night. Even when we do get it on a regular basis, there are peaks and valleys in our performance and satisfaction. Though sex with your steady guy may diminish from the level on which it started, it shouldn't ever feel routine.

Just keep in mind that we are not claiming to be sex experts. We're not psychologists either. But we are guys who have been in relationships where sex has sizzled out completely. No guy will pop the question when he feels that there is no spark at all left with the woman with whom he's living or monogamous. We want to share with you some of the things we think will keep that passion alive in your committed relationship.

Speak

We know you may have heard it before, but the one thing that can save your relationship in the bedroom is communication. The difference between good sexual relationships and poor ones lies in the communication between the two parties. The importance of listening to your man and telling him what you want only increases as you move beyond the first wave of passion that brought you two together. You have to share with your man what you like to do in bed and vice versa. You also have to be willing to spice up your love life by vocalizing your responses to what your boyfriend does or asking him what he likes just so he has the chance to verbalize what he wants.

You must understand that the turn-on for your man is not all about how your lips feel as you kiss his lips, how his nipples feel as you circle them with your tongue, or how smoothly your hand works his genitals. These things may feel great, but there's much more to a fulfilling sex life than mechanics. In our experience, the quality of sex is based on the psychology of it all. You need to know what gets your man going—is it a teasing approach, a submissive approach, a dominant approach, or some other way of relating to each other in the bedroom? Then respond with the appropriate verbal additions to your activities such as:

TEASING: Is this how you want it, like this? I could just stop, or I could touch you very lightly, like this. What if I don't want to. I could just walk away. What would you do then?

SUBMISSIVE: I'm yours. Do what you want, anything you want. Take me.

DOMINANT: Give it to me. Harder. Oh, yeah, baby. Fill me up. How deep can you go?

Many men like a variety of different approaches for different nights. It's up to you to discover what your man really wants. We are just telling you that his satisfaction has a great deal to do with what you say, how you act, the speed with which you respond to his requests, the way you move your body—everything. Everyone is different and people have different levels of sexual relations that they deem kinky or out of bounds. We are obviously not here to explore all of the options available, just to give you some ideas about how you can remain open to your man.

Of course, every man likes to hear a good compliment (or an entire list of them) during lovemaking. We don't know any man who would not like to hear, "You're the best." Keep your man's ego in mind in bed. He will appreciate you for it.

Listen—It's Better Than Knowing Every Trick in the Book

How many times have we been in bed with a woman who thinks she knows all the tricks? When we try to tell her to do something a little different, she then resorts to another method from her repertoire. She acts as if we don't know what pleases us the most. She seems to think she has a better idea for solving the problem at hand. How ridiculous is that? This kind of woman—the one who has many skills on autopilot—can be frustrating to a man in bed. When we encounter women like this, or hear about them, we wonder why they need or want a partner at all.

You don't want to be perceived as the sexual Ms. Know-It-All when you are embarking on a committed relationship. This frame of mind could lose you Mr. Right. First off, he will wonder how many men you have been with to learn what you have. Second, he'll feel like what he says or wants comes second to your need to dominate the bed. We're not saying that we expect our Ms. Rights to be naive or submissive at all. When it comes to our long-term partners, we just want to be in an interactive relationship, one in which our opinions are heard, acknowledged as important, and responded to sensitively.

That is why we stress communication. If you watch porno films or read the *Kama Sutra,* you can see that there are a limited number of sexual positions. Nearly every woman is capable of engaging in sex in these different ways. So you will not be "better" than the other lovers your man has had just because you know all these positions. If you are inexperienced, or if you have just been traditional in your sexual practices, don't worry. The best thing you can have when you are in bed with your long-term love is an open ear. Listen to what he is really saying, and don't be scared to ask questions. Your man will appreciate that he can teach you something and be flattered that you are really hearing him and are open to trying out what he feels like doing in bed. He will be reassured that you won't be afraid to try something new in the future, and he will think about all the variety he can have in bed with one woman, the right woman, you!

Details, Details

The three of us agree that it's the details of sex that really turn us on. Okay, we won't deny that, to a man, the simple, unadorned act of placing his penis in any woman's vagina feels good. With all of our other senses muffled, we're sure we'd probably like that sensation alone. Though that scenario might thrill us once or thrill us slightly many times, it won't be enough to sustain our interest over the long haul in a committed relationship.

We want a sexual experience filled with memorable details—words, feelings, sounds, smells, and tastes. We want our sex life with a committed woman to be one of many sensual pleasures. If we can't have a variety of women, we want a variety of sensations. We want surprises and spontaneity. We want you to add your part. We want to have fun. We want to play.

Let's take an example. You are in bed with your boyfriend and he moans, "Let me see your ass." Your next move should not just be to let him get a better view of your rear end. Instead you should say, "You like my ass, huh?" Whatever he appears to like—accentuate it. Allow him to use all of his senses, enable him to enjoy all stimuli and use his imagination.

The point is this. When we say something or suggest something in bed, we hope you'll join in the fun. We are not going to spell out everything for you—that would make the interaction much less interesting and exciting. If we spell out every little detail, sex seems rehearsed to us. We want to be able just to hint at where we'd like to go and have you pick up the ball and run with it. We know this can be fairly difficult at the beginning, as you are not a mind reader. We would hope you would like the challenge of introducing a little of the unknown into a long-term sexual relationship. Ultimately, we want you to follow us into our fantasies and play a part—add details that we would find powerful turn-ons.

Follow Him to His Fantasy Land

A man's fantasies are powerful and need to be indulged. Of course, a woman's fantasies are just as important. As controlling, powerful, and verbose as your boyfriend may be, he may still not let you in on his fantasies. You have to try and get into his head. Raise the issue of sexual fantasies. By doing so, let your man know that he can open up to you. Reassure him that you will not make fun of his thoughts or preferences. Follow up on this conversation during foreplay with your boyfriend. Introduce a theme he's mentioned to you when you discussed sexual fantasies or, if he was silent then, see if he'll share anything as you both get revved up. While your man may not be forthcoming at first, we guarantee he has fantasies and, eventually, you'll be able to coax them out of him. Once he has shared them with you, make him glad he did by bringing them alive in the bedroom.

Allowing a man to indulge in his fantasies or merely act them out while being with you is a surefire way of attaching yourself to him for life. He may not come clean right away with all of his fantasies. Instead, he may share them every so often. Don't ignore what he does tell you. That will damage your sexual relationship with him. He will think that you don't care what he needs or wants, or are embarrassed by his preferences. Be sure to use the information he shares. Don't let this powerful information pass you by without acting on it.

Your man might be cautious about sharing his interior world of sexual thoughts with you at first, afraid of how vulnerable he feels when he divulges them. He may never have told another woman about what goes on in his head in quite the same way. He may be concerned that you will laugh at him. Once he sees that you are a companion who is willing to explore his fantasies, then your man will open up to you even further. This cycle of growing trust and revelation will be what ensures that you have a sex life that is forever new and interesting. This is just what you want in a long-term relationship with a man. When a man shares his sexual fantasies with you, he is giving you the chance of being his "dream" in bed. If you hear what he says and expound on the concept, he will never let you go.

The only thing we will caution you against is including any others in the sexual fantasies you and your boyfriend share. No matter what he says, don't allow anyone else into this special relationship of trust that you have built with each other. Your man may suggest you invite others into your bedroom, but you should never, ever take him up on it. A committed relationship means you and your man have sex only with each other.

We all know the power sex has in our relationships. We have all seen relationships end because of a lackluster sex life. Everything else can be terrific—but if the sex is dull or non-existent, the relationship cannot last. Sex seems simple enough at first glance, but it is probably the most complex area of a relationship. This is especially true when it comes to committed men because we always have in the backs of our minds the fact that if we marry you, we will not be able to have sex with any other woman. If your man finds that you are open to variety and you make him feel comfortable enough to share his fantasies, you are helping to ensure that he will want you with him for life as his wife.

What's This Two-Woman Fantasy Anyway?

Let's take a look at lesbianism and why it is so enticing to men. That's right, we said it! Lesbianism. Why do we bring up lesbianism here? Because so many women have asked us, "What's the deal with men and their attraction to two women getting it on?" We feel that we need to uncover the truths and myths behind this fantasy that many men have.

Let's just be frank—men *love* lesbianism. We can't get enough of it. Of course, we don't really mean lesbianism among lesbians. We mean two beautiful women who come together in a sexual act that is a performance on display in a porno movie, magazine, or strip club. "Lesbianism" is the word men use to describe this fantasy image of two women making love to one another for the benefit of an audience. We realize it's quite a different representation from the reality of most lesbian women. We know that real lesbian women would have no interest in us.

So you ask, what is it about "lesbianism" that turns us on? Women have told us that they don't often find male homosexuality to be erotic. So, why is lesbianism so erotic to us—straight professional men contemplating long-term commitment?

For a heterosexual man, "lesbianism" is an unusual behavior to observe. The average man doesn't get much of an opportunity to see this type of sexual interaction very often except in porno films. Not what we are used to seeing in our daily lives, the image is continually fresh for us. It is a double scoop of female eroticism with a naughty, titillating twist.

We are also intrigued to see women doing to women what we are used to doing to women. The tenderness, sensuality, and attention to detail that women lend to the act of making love is arousing for us to watch. The fact that there is no male image in the way for us to compete with in the lesbian scenario must also be part of the attraction this act has for us. From what we can tell, we as men project ourselves into this slow and sensuous act that goes on between two women and revel in the sensations that would come our way if we could join them. Our opinion is that one woman is good, but two are even better. We love that the only male in the picture is us—we are free to take any fantasy role we like—participant or imaginative observer!

The Threesome

Well, that explains why men like watching lesbianism, but let's take the next logical step (at least from a man's point of view)—and discuss the fantasy of partaking in a threesome. Of course, we mean two women and one man, what else? Wow, our collective heads explode at just the thought of it. The image of two women in bed with him will put a smile on any man's face. Yes, even your man's, if he's frank.

If we get turned on as men just being able to watch two women "go at it," imagine how excited we would become if we could take part in the picture. Where lesbianism provides us with a fantasy, a threesome would allow us to do just that—be part of the action in real life. When we are watching lesbianism in porno we think we know it. But when we see two women going at it in person it is even more erotic. The more intimate they get the more we like it. Two women pleasing each other and us—that's off the charts.

This is how a man thinks when you mention a threesome. A man would immediately envision two women working on him at the same time. Two mouths, four hands, twenty fingers, there's plenty to work with. You might say, "Well, there's only one penis." A man would say, "No problem, there's enough here for two—share!" The two different mouths and styles are so erotic for a man to contemplate. He can imagine reaching a high level of ecstasy—maybe the highest possible. Needless to say, these thoughts of a threesome are very, very pleasing for the male ego.

What does this have to do with you? First off, you cannot provide lesbianism for your man. The professional man does not really look at lesbianism as a fine quality in a woman he is thinking of marrying. Again, we know this view is both very politically incorrect and hypocritical after what we have told you—but it is truthful nonetheless. The professional man looks at lesbians the same way he looks at strippers. They're very, very exciting—but not for the long term.

As much as we love lesbianism, we would not want our significant other to take part in it. As we have explained, it is an incredible turn-on for men to watch lesbianism and have the chance to participate with two women in a threesome, but, ultimately, we don't want to marry women who make this activity a part of their lives. If you want to be in a relationship for the long term, then don't involve yourself in lesbianism. And don't discuss it with your man. If you even show a little interest in it, he will have short-term interest in you.

Like it or not, the professional man is looking for the "good girl" to settle down with and to marry. He doesn't want to take any chances when it comes to his future. He has worked so hard during school and his professional life that he is not going to jeopardize his reputation by marrying a "wild woman." Wild women have too many risks associated with them for professional men to pursue them for committed, long-term relationships. And for some strange psychological reason, men look at lesbians and bisexuals as "wild women."

You ladies may read this and say, "Hey, this is a trap!" You're right, it is a trap. We aren't kidding either. Men are highly excited by women on women, two women on us. Never take an interest in watching lesbian porno or engage in this type of activity with your professional man and another woman. Don't even utter the fact that you yourself think it is interesting. If you even let on that you once French-kissed your best girlfriend in a nightclub one drunken night to get a psycho guy away from you, he will look at you in a different light. That light isn't a flattering light either. If you allude to any interest in another woman sexually ever, even in a humorous way, your man will feel threatened. Thoughts of you not focusing on him and his sexual appeal or even leaving him for another woman will creep into your boyfriend's head and be impossible to unseat.

There may be that temptation for you to succumb to satisfying your boyfriend's threesome desires. He may try to convince you that he will love you more if you partake in such an intimate scene. *Don't be fooled.* Don't give in. If he loves you, this letdown of never having the chance with two women at once will not ruin your relationship. If he doesn't love you, making love with him and another woman simultaneously will not cause him to love you. Essentially it comes down to one basic concept. If a man loves a woman, he wants her for himself. Yeah, there are a lot of scenarios that excite us, however, those are best left to pornos and the imagination or to be enjoyed during the single life at best.

The Great Temptation

The struggle, the torture, the battle. A new woman. The girl down the block. The woman across the hall. The tall one in the office. The video rental store employee who wears tight shirts. The temptation. We act as if we could get these women at the snap of a finger. Maybe we can and maybe we can't—regardless, we still want 'em.

We figured it would be a good idea to relate to you how we stop ourselves from this great temptation of other women when we are in a committed relationship. First off, we try to commit ourselves to women whom we find sexually exciting and who are comfortable and confident enough to be open in bed, ensuring us years of fun sex.

The three of us also agree that we try not to think too much about the obvious single-partner effect of being in a committed relationship for the long term. We try to get a certain perspective on the one woman for life, one sex partner for life, that helps us see the benefits involved.

For instance, Brad does not look at marriage as a life without other women. That would be a terrible, glass-half-empty perspective. Instead, Brad focuses on the added joy marriage to Cheryl brings to his life day-by-day. He keeps his sights on the here and now. The sole-sex-partner way of life seems less overwhelming to him when he thinks this way. It's a frame of mind that's not much different from being an alcoholic and trying to quit drinking by taking life one day at a time. As alcoholics are addicted to alcohol, most men are addicted to conquering many women. Looking at the short term makes the end of his era of sexual conquests much more bearable. It doesn't sound like a nice way to put it, but again, this is reality inside your man's head. You've never heard it before, but we'd bet a great deal on that fact that this is the way he thinks.

Another way men stay faithful in their committed relationships is that they avoid, or at least reduce, the "dangerous situations" they place themselves in once they find that special woman they are considering spending the rest of their lives with. For example, now that Rich is engaged to Marla, he clearly avoids those long nights out on the town—with the guys, the drinking, and the women. His single life was a long string of those nights. He enjoyed partying and painting the town red with his friends, but now that's not where Rich wants to be. Those nights have served their purpose. They brought him to Marla. Now, his personal life has a different focus than rowdy fun with the guys. His focus is Marla. Like Rich, a smart man weans himself off the crazy single life while he is courting his soon-to-be wife, so he is able to remain faithful. It's a change in lifestyle, sure, but one he wants.

A friend of ours, who did not date a great deal when he was single, just got married. Until recently, parties and clubbing were not a big part of his life. During the past two years he has taken up weight lifting to assist him in landing parts as an actor. As he accomplished his goal of buffing up, our friend liked the new attention he was getting from women at the gym. To ride that energy of fawning women more often, he began going out at night with friends and business colleagues. Well, needless to say, he looks great and his professional life is flourishing—but his marriage is suffering. He confided in one of us and said that the temptation out there is incredible. Of course it is. That is why we agree that a great coping strategy is avoidance.

You may have noticed that your boyfriend, fiancé, or husband also stopped wanting to go to clubs and bars once you began to get serious. Why? you ask. Because he doesn't want to see what else is out there. He wants to begin curbing his appetite for that lifestyle.

Men who constantly place themselves in compromising situations, like going out often to parties with many single friends, are asking for trouble. We've seen a committed man crumble before the temptation of another woman too many times not to warn you of this behavior. We're not saying that you shouldn't let your guy go out with his single friends. He will always maintain contact with many of them. When you start to see your man starting to slow down the "single man's" life, you know that he is preparing himself for complete commitment.

A man who is seriously dating a woman begins to let his friends become just that—"friends." Not his life. *You* become his life. It's a slow, gradual process in which your guy will switch gears. When he does this, give him positive reinforcement. Don't make fun of him, with comments suggesting that he is becoming an old man. Ladies, you have a choice here—a quieter, less-tempted man who is committed to you, or a single man who can't stop chasing skirts and will never settle down.

It reminds us of when we were young and our parents would make sure we were hanging around with the right friends, fearing that the wrong ones would be a bad influence. Well, bad influences are what guys who want to stay in good relationships avoid. And believe us, there are many bad influences out there.

Keep in mind that a committed man can and will go out with his friends from time to time. When your man is committed and happy in the relationship, he will avoid temptation. Don't worry, he's not turning into an old fart—he's in love. Encourage him to maintain his friendships and happily observe the lack of desire that he has to go out and party it up. This move from a dating scene toward you is the last and final sign that your guy is really ready to settle down. It is the logical order of things. It happened to Rich and Brad and it will happen to your Mr. Right, too.

The Short Story on Penis Size

All women need to know about this topic. Penis size. You've thought about it. You've talked about it with your girlfriends. We know you've read about surveys in your favorite magazines. But this time you are going to hear what penis size means to a man from men (well-endowed men, of course—what man would say otherwise?).

To begin with, all men harbor some insecurity about their own penis size. Maybe one guy is twelve inches long erect, but he isn't happy about how it looks flaccid. The next guy is thick but short. And the next is—well, you get the picture. In some ways the penis is like any other body part to anyone. There are good points and bad ones. If you studied any body part as much as guys study their penises, you would find something wrong with it, too.

A man's penis is a very special body part. Most women think that it is special to a man because he *receives* pleasure with it, but they are wrong. It is special to most men because with it they *give* pleasure. You see, any guy can receive pleasure with his penis. Short, long, thin, thick—no problem. The reason guys are insecure about penis size is that we think that it may alter our ability to pleasure a woman.

What we are going to say next is without doubt the most important advice in the book. *Never comment in any way about your man's penis being small.* Don't joke about it, don't imply it, don't let it fly when you're furious, and don't ever let him believe that you ever thought it. Never, never, never. If you do, the relationship is over. If you make any reference to the smallness of his penis, your guy thinks, "I can't give her pleasure," and it's over. He will always think that in your eyes he has a small penis, and he's sexually inadequate. He will resent you forever and ever. The relationship cannot last.

Even if your guy does have a small penis, he doesn't want to suffer by comparison to other men's penis sizes. Your man's ego is fragile. As long as he thinks his small penis isn't a problem for you—and it should not be a problem if you really love him—everything should be fine. Just don't draw attention to it. Meticulously avoid even the most remote or vague reference to it. Don't even think about it.

We are going to go one step farther here. Also, be careful about saying your man has a large penis. If you say he is big, he will think you are lying (unless he is about twelve inches long or longer when erect). That is an example of how obsessed we are with our own penises. If you say we are small, we hate you. If you say we are big, we don't believe you. You can't win, right? It gets worse.

Don't ever comment about your old boyfriend's penis. Don't mention anything about it. If your significant other brings it up for some perverted reason, tell him you forgot your ex even had a penis or that it's just a blurry haze in your memory. Don't get pulled into a discussion about particulars. You won't win the discussion even if your new boyfriend's penis is twice the size of your last boyfriend's. If you want a chance at long-term love with your new man, don't take the bait. Your boyfriend, fiancé, or husband will be too macho to admit most of this, but he will be glad if you follow all of our advice. Believe us.

Every guy wants a long, large, thick penis. Some guys have one that other guys would dream of having, but don't think they do. The funny thing is that all men would just like about one more inch in their pants. We don't have wild delusions. We are reasonable in our requests. Just one more inch. We know how sex is with our own penis. It is good. She moves, moans, and tells us how good we are. Imagine how good it would be for her with another inch added on. She would be in ecstasy!

Understand, one more inch doesn't add to our sexual pleasure but our girlfriend's. We would like to know how it feels to make her more excited. How a man performs in bed

is more a function of his ego at work than his desire for sexual gratification. Being good in bed and feeling we are great
in bed make us feel more powerful. We men need power in
order to be in happy, long-term relationships. Remember
that this type of power that comes from performing well in
bed does not conflict with your needs as women in bed. In
fact, the more we seem to please you, the better we feel.
Wow, are we ever insecure, right?

Now you don't have to read all those women's magazines
to understand your man and his penis. You know, regardless
of size, his penis causes every man to worry. Maybe it's not a
worry for every man, but let's call it a concern. By the way,
this is one area that is definitely not specific to the "professional man." This goes for the professional man, the blue-
collar man, and every man in between.

Breasts: Does Size Matter to Men?

Speaking of body parts, many women have written us with
questions and concerns about their breast size and how men
respond to it. Do men want women with large breasts? Are
big-breasted women more likely to find Mr. Right than
small-breasted women? Why do guys like large breasts?
There are lots of questions about breasts. And we're here to
answer them.

What do we like—big breasts or small? Both! Some guys
have a particular preference for a certain breast size, some
don't; it really depends on the guy. The one thing we three
agree on is that proportion is very important—a woman
should have breasts that match the rest of her body propor-
tionally.

Here is the best news. Breasts really don't make a man

want to marry a woman. Even if he is a "breast man," he can of course marry a woman with a small chest if she is "the right one." Yes, this is true. We know you think that some men would never marry a woman with small breasts, but that is not the case. We know a number of "breast men" who have become serious with and married women who have smaller than average chests.

Our opinion is that women are more caught up with the breast thing than men. We thought about it and guessed that women talk about breasts more than men do. We only talk about the breast issue when we come face to face with an especially good or unusual pair of them. What we mean is this. When a large-breasted woman walks by us we stare or comment on her. But that's it. When she turns the corner, she's out of our minds. Men see and appreciate women's bodies even after they are committed to one woman—this is known as "the look but don't touch axiom." Women's breasts are a very apparent part of a woman. Even when a woman is fully clothed, the silhouette of her breasts is there for all to see. This causes more men to look, which causes women with small breasts to become insecure. So you can blame yourselves when it comes to this.

You see, we men are luckier. We imagine that you are probably just as insecure about your breasts as we are about our penises, but our private parts are kept private all day. Your chest is exposed, thereby making it, shall we say, a bigger issue. How terrible it would be if we had to walk around with our penises out and women would judge us by the size. Men would be devastated. We feel for you in this regard.

A woman will, of course, receive more general male attention if she has extremely large breasts, but, in the end, she may never land a professional man. The professional man is a special breed. We do not want to be embarrassed. Business dinners, company picnics, parties—we do not want to have a porno star on our arm. That would be very embarrassing, and it's not what we are looking for long term. And long term is what this book's about. Don't get us wrong, women with big breasts are appealing. We love to look. We love to touch. But sometimes women accentuate their breasts, and it becomes a little freaky. Bigger is not necessarily better. A man doesn't necessarily want to marry a woman who has especially big breasts. He might even think that such a well-endowed girl is better for a one night stand instead of a long-term committed relationship.

When it comes to body parts on women, all parts get equal points. There really is no added value for the large breasts. Based on many conversations with women, it seems that you think that your man may run off with any woman who has larger breasts than you do. We're here to tell you that you have this all wrong. Yes, breasts are an enticing female body part a man can often clearly see outlined, but a pleasant face, pretty hair, and a nicely curved rear end are all features that attract men as well.

For instance, Brad is an "ass man" and always has been. He has never ever been very impressed by women with large breasts. His motto has always been "a woman with a nice ass usually has a nice stomach and pretty legs as well." So there you go, not all men are fixated on breasts. Don't get us wrong, we know many guys who love women with larger breasts, but these guys would never replace a woman with an engaging personality and striking face with a less interesting, less attractive woman with a bigger chest.

Before we end the section on breasts, we must address the topic of breast implants. The three of us agree that good implants seem as good as real breasts. Moderate breast augmentation is fine—if a woman feels strongly that she should have such work done and she's in the hands of a reputable physician. Why not? But we do laugh at those explosive breasts some women have implanted. Those women will be spectacles for as long as they keep the breasts. Women who choose such a front are not for the professional man. Again, we don't want to be seen or associated with a grotesque, out-of-proportion embarrassment.

Remember, getting breast implants will not make a man commit to you. Breast size has no effect on the long-term relationship. Your chest may be something that initially attracts a man to you, but in terms of getting a man to commit to a long-term relationship, rest assured that breast size has nothing to do with it.

Your Prior Sexual History

Prior sexual history is a catch-22. We don't want to know how many guys you slept with nor do we want to know with whom you've slept, but we also *must* know. We don't want to know because an otherwise perfect woman whom we want to marry could be cut off the list because she slept with too many guys, or the one wrong guy. But how do we really know the person we marry without knowing how she's conducted her sexual life and with whom?

As we will explain, regardless of what your experience is, if the number of guys you've slept with is high, then you should lie. If there is a guy or guys with whom you have slept that you think your boyfriend would be horrified to find out about, don't tell him.

You may say, why is this so important? Well, we don't want to walk around with, introduce our family and coworkers to, or marry a woman who is a tramp. Harsh? We don't think it is. Men protect themselves when it comes to the women they include in their lives for the long term. Our greatest fear in life is going out to dinner with our new wife and having three guys in the restaurant giggling because they slept with her at some time in the past. It doesn't matter that she is with us now. That is a non-issue. We are very sensitive about our serious girlfriends and wives. We let them see a very vulnerable side of us. We don't want other men to know what goes on with the women we are committed to. We want to protect our most intimate relationships and want to be confident that what goes on there is private and will remain so. An intimate relationship is the soft underbelly of our masculinity and we don't want it exposed.

Formula for Acceptable Sexual Partner Quantity

When women hear us say these things they usually want to know how many sexual partners is too many. To answer this question we developed a formula—we solicited the help of a person with a Ph.D. in calculus in its development. This formula works for all women of all ages. It goes like this:

Take the number of years over sixteen you are. For instance, if you are twenty-five years old, you are nine years over sixteen. Multiply that number by twelve. Take the total and divide that number by twenty-one. You got it. That's how many guys are acceptable for you to sleep with. But here's the catch. If your total exceeds ten, then cap the guys you have slept with at ten. You heard us, *lie*. You must lie. No man likes to think of his woman sleeping with another guy, much less ten other guys. So, this formula doesn't mean that you all are entitled to sleep with ten men and should go out and fill this as if it were a quota.

Let's take a look at what kind of numbers this formula would produce depending on your age. Remember you can round up pursuant to normal mathematical rules of rounding decimals. However, when you get to ten, that's the top limit of acceptable partners.

Age	Acceptable Partners
21	2.86
22	3.43
23	4
24	4.75
25	5.14
26	5.71
27	6.29
28	6.86
29	7.43
30	8
31	8.57
32	9.14
33	9.71
34	10
35	10

This formula helps women to understand what is the acceptable number of guys they can sleep with. If you are reading this book and you have a daughter we suggest that you give the book to her so she can begin working with the numbers early. This will enable her to plan ahead.

The Prostitute Formula

We have one other formula. The Prostitute Formula. If your age equals or is less than the number of guys you have had sex with, then you are a prostitute in a man's eyes. In these formulas, you *do not* exclude spring break trips, Club Med trips, or the college years; orgies *do not* count as one (you must count every guy in the room). Start calculating!

We believe that certain things are better left unsaid, but it is inevitable that we will want to know about your past. If we are moving toward a commitment with you, we will ask. Be prepared. If you have slept with just a few guys, check the acceptable partner number for your age above to see if it falls on or below that number. If so, tell the truth about your number of sexual partners when your boyfriend asks. If your number of sexual partners is high—whether just above the accepted number or close to the prostitute definition—we really believe that you should lie. Use the formula we have supplied and provide the number for your age. Cap the number at ten no matter what. We can't handle the truth. Too large a number will compel us to break up with you. Our egos won't permit us to live the rest of our lives thinking we have gone where all men have gone before. We know we said that honesty is the best policy, but women—draw the line here.

There's one last stumbling block to complete honesty. *You cannot talk about any details regarding your intimate relationships with past guys.* You think that is an obvious piece of advice, but it isn't. You'd be surprised what women say and how sensitive we are. For instance, you are Chris's girl-friend, and you are arguing because you slept with a guy Chris knows before you started going out with him. While you two are arguing, you mention that you "only slept with him a few times." *Oh, boy,* does that hurt. You just escalated the argument. Women might say that this is just a "detail." We didn't ask for details. We don't want details like this—ever. The man's psyche is incredibly sensitive to these sexual details—sexual details like these stick to our minds like glue. A small comment about an intimate act with a guy other than ourselves confirms and paints the one picture that we don't want in our minds—the picture of you with other guy(s). The clearer that picture gets the less of a chance we will marry you.

Rich once went out with a woman who felt that it was appropriate to tell a story about her and a bunch of guys on a boat. Well, she said, things got wild on the boat and she was the center of attention, so to speak. This was, as she described it, her wildest sexual experience. She didn't go into great detail, but this sketch of an image was enough to keep her in Rich's "good for now" girl list and forever out of his "wife potential" category. If she wants to ever get married, she'd better keep that story to herself in the future.

Women seem to get themselves in trouble early on. In our experience, during the third or fourth date women become a little more open with the conversation they have with a man, and sometimes they think it is safe to talk about past sexual experiences. The two of you know each other. You feel com-fortable with each other. You figure, "what the hell?" Maybe you tell a possible Mr. Right that you once went out with a guy whose penis was so large it hurt you when you had sex with him. We are here to tell you that because you told this guy that story, he cannot marry you. We can't begin to describe what will be going through that guy's mind. Yes, it's that easy to ruin your chance at marriage with the professional guy of your dreams. Be careful. Keep your racy stories to yourself.

Remember you want to get married. You must think ahead. What you do and say today can and will affect you later. You never know which guy will be The One. So don't say something that a man will never be able to get out of his mind. Look to the future with the guys that you date. It may seem silly now, but one wrong anecdote may damage or completely destroy your chances of long-term commitment and marriage. Be circumspect—you never know which guy will be your Mr. Right.

7

—

THE FIRST BIG STEP: FROM CASUAL DATING TO MONOGAMY

We are now ready to explain the specific thoughts that go through a man's mind when he wants to commit to you. For a man there are actually two levels of commitment to a woman: commitment to monogamy and commitment to engagement. This chapter will focus on a man's commitment to you as his one girlfriend. In Chapter 10 we'll explore the move to the second level—engagement. Getting a man to commit to monogamy is no small feat. Once you know how your guy approaches this first level of real commitment, you will have a much better chance of getting him there with you.

What Is Commitment and Why Are Men So Afraid of It?

The word commitment can take on many different meanings when it comes to settling down with a woman. It might mean a concerted, guaranteed, all-out effort to get laid and settle down with a woman . . . in bed. This usually comes during the dating stages and that is what *What Men Want* is all about. As relationships progress and mature, we like to look at commitment as an evolution or a process. Commitment is not something men want to be reminded of nor do we ever want to admit that we are in fact committed. For a man, becoming committed is like going through a maze with a blindfold on. He has an innate sense that what he is doing is right because it feels so good. He isn't afraid to get to the other side, and deep down he wants to get there. He enjoys the new feeling of being somewhere he has never been, and he gets intense gratification from making the right moves, basically by instinct and by going with the flow. The transition from an uncommitted man playing the field to a man considering lifelong commitment is a gradual calculated process. A man moving toward committed status makes decisions carefully and cautiously over a long period of time. As a man gets positive reinforcement or gratification from his girlfriend for each move he makes toward monogamy, he will feel more and more comfortable making the decision to take the relationship to the next level.

Men don't want to feel they are smack in the middle of a challenging process that requires hard work. They don't want to be reminded of the uncertainty of reaching the other side. The thought of possibly being rejected by the women they love makes them feel very vulnerable. They can sense the great potential for pain they face when this thought arises. They'd rather not think about it; they'd rather keep the blindfold on.

From experience, men know that women tend to like to talk about the progress of the relationship and hurry it on its way toward marriage. In effect, they want to rip that blindfold right off their boyfriends with talks about "us," "the relationship," or even worse, "the time line." Instead of moving the relationship to another level, talks like these can set it back or bring it to an end. The fact is that the more men are reminded that they are in a committed relationship, the easier it is for them to bail out. When they have "the talk" their girlfriends force, men's fears—of never being able to experience the pleasure that comes with meeting someone new or never being with another woman for the first time again—come right to the surface.

This may sound immature. We know that it may not be what you want to hear. But it is true. Being with many women makes a man feel good about himself. It is a huge ego boost. Sensing that this particular form of ego boost could disappear forever, men get really scared. Stricken by panic, they forget how much they love the woman in front of them or on the other end of the telephone line. They feel out of control. Trying to get back to that comfortable place, where they are in control and out of danger, men will try to cut the conversation or even the relationship short. Their strongest impulse is to dash for the nearest exit and be out of the "maze" as quickly as possible.

His Commitment to Monogamy

As a relationship progresses through the first year of dating and a man feels that the woman he is with is in the "marriage material" girl category, he will move toward monogamy. This is not a conscious decision—he doesn't just wake up one day and say, "Okay. That's it, no more strange women. Throw out the black book, the Barry White CDs, and take the mirror off the ceiling. No more dating for me." For a man, deciding to be monogamous is more of a state of mind. He thinks to himself, This woman makes me incredibly happy, and I can see falling in love with her. I don't need to look elsewhere for other women. I don't need to satisfy my fragile ego and sleep with many women to feel good about myself. My girlfriend provides me with all I need, and therefore I will not look elsewhere or be with anyone else.

How long should it take for your man to decide to be monogamous? you may wonder. We think you should date a maximum of three years before getting engaged. That usually means roughly two years of dating and one year of living together. So, about the one-year mark of dating is when we think a man might seriously consider monogamy. This is a general time frame, we don't suggest that you rush into anything—but we also don't want you to get strung along, waiting forever. Each couple's relationship moves at its own speed, some get closer more quickly and others take a little longer.

Let your relationship develop and evolve naturally. Whatever you do—don't pressure your man to move faster than he's ready to by asking him where the relationship is going, when you're going to get engaged, or when you're going to get married. As we've told you, this could be devastating to a very healthy relationship that is well on its way to engagement and marriage. As we discussed in *What Men Want,* this is a crucial period of the relationship. You must know how to "nurture Mr. Right."

If you have been dating a guy for some time and feel you are being taken for a ride even after you've applied the advice in this book, then you might well be. If this is the case, don't waste your time putting pressure on the guy you're seeing to get serious or commit. That approach will only prolong your agony and his. Get out of the relationship.

We don't want to give you a false sense of security here. At this point, you still are not guaranteed the ring. Sure, he probably tells you he loves you, and he has committed to being monogamous with you, but this is a very tricky stage during which many promising relationships fall apart. There are many reasons for a breakup at this juncture; some are the man's fault, some are the woman's fault, others are neither person's fault, just simply a matter of circumstances. We can guarantee that a man must go through this gradual process and must first commit to being monogamous before he will be comfortable taking the relationship to the next level.

How do you know if a man has reached the "Commitment to Monogamy" level? Can you ask him? Will he tell you? Are there signs you can read to know that he is "yours" and only "yours"? As you know, we do advocate open and honest communication. In fact, it is essential. We believe that there's a fine line between open communication (including your right to know where you stand in the relationship and where the relationship is going) and bringing up topics that men don't like to discuss. The signals men send out in relationships are the key indicators of their feelings about the woman and the direction in which the relationship is going. When it comes to judging your man's commitment level, you must focus on his actions. You've probably heard this before—from your boyfriend. But don't get angry and upset yet. We aren't going to leave you with that comment alone, as he probably does.

Rich is a good example of a guy who showed signs of being committed to Marla during their three years of dating. The goal of becoming a doctor kept Rich extremely busy, but he was looking for Ms. Right and when he met Marla, he knew she was that special woman with wife potential whom he had hoped to find. He prayed she would have the patience to stick with him as he made it through his residency and found his first job. He took her to expensive dinners early in their courtship and planned special weekends away whenever he could find time in his schedule. The first year of dating went by and Rich knew that Marla would love to move in, but he didn't feel she should until he was more comfortable in his role at the hospital. What Rich did do, which only a committed man would do, was help Marla out as she worked to achieve her own goals. He picked her up from work in downtown Philadelphia and took her to her night business classes at Villanova where she was getting her MBA so she didn't have to wait for the bus. When Marla had to study, Rich brought dinner over from their favorite Chinese place or cooked for her himself. When she wanted to go shopping on a Saturday, Rich would come directly from his shift at the hospital and take Marla to the mall to get what she needed. During days when their schedules didn't give them time to meet, Rich often called Marla to tell her he loved her and sent her chocolates and flowers to show her he was thinking of her.

In short, if possible Rich always made time in his busy days to be there for Marla when she needed him. He not only took her out on dates and bought her gifts but he spent much of his precious free time helping her with chores, cooking, or studying. No busy professional man would do such things for a woman unless he was seriously interested in her. A man may take a "good for now" girl out for a pricey dinner and bring her some flowers, but you will never catch him picking up her laundry, going shopping with her, fixing her leaky faucet, or greeting her at the airport after a business trip.

Our women friends tell us they are often unable to read their guys' signals, and are frustrated trying to decipher their intentions. In the dark about what is really going on in their relationships, they ask us to interpret what their men are thinking and feeling by describing how their men act. No doubt you could use the same pointers we've given them. Here are some clues that will help you see what your man's behavior means—and the reasons behind it. What follows might sound like common sense, but we are convinced that it is common sense not often applied. You can be the judge.

Everything's Great, Until . . .

Think about the beginning of your relationship. You were probably dating your potential Mr. Right once or twice a week. Several months went by before he asked you out for prime time—a Friday or Saturday night. When you started seeing him on the weekends, you knew your relationship was getting more serious and so did he. Until then he had been keeping his options open and meeting other women on the weekends. This is a man's pattern for easing into a relationship with a woman who has wife potential. Even if he knows you're a "marriage material" girl who could be Ms. Right from the first day, a man won't jump into a relationship, especially a monogamous relationship, very quickly.

Men start out dating casually and get more serious gradually. As your own relationships progressed, you probably found that you and your guy were spending more time together. You know, the romantic Saturday nights at a nice candlelight dinner in a dark, cozy restaurant. He ordered a good bottle of your favorite pinot grigio. You spent the entire night gazing into each other's eyes and talking about how happy you both were and how excited you were about your upcoming vacation together. The night progressed and you went back to his place, where you had been spending the night regularly. What followed? Great passionate sex, of course. You fell asleep snugly in the spoon position. Perhaps in the morning you had great sex again, despite the mutual bad breath. Finally, the two of you headed out for a bite and continued to spend the entire Sunday just being with each other. At this stage in the relationship, you most likely had met one another's family and maybe even discussed your future together.

Now what type of picture have we painted? One of a committed, monogamous, healthy relationship, right? Yet women are often completely baffled by what happens next. The work week starts and the man gets engulfed in his job. He is no longer able to be completely attentive to you as he was throughout the weekend. Monday and Tuesday he's faced with a busy schedule at the office and does not return home from work until eleven o'clock at night. He hardly has time to think and hasn't called you, his girlfriend. He doesn't pick up the phone to call you until Wednesday but as he does he is looking forward to speaking with you and seeing you again soon. In these two and a half days, you have become very insecure about the relationship. You simply *must* ask him "Where is this relationship going?" Come on, think back, we know you have probably done this before—you can admit it.

Judging from the thousands of e-mails and letters we have received from women who have found themselves in this exact situation, this string of events is all too common. What women do not see is that there is no problem here—as far as the man is concerned. The man in question feels good about the serious, committed, monogamous relationship he finds himself in and is demonstrating his feelings with his actions and time spent with his girlfriend over the weekend. On Monday, he may want to be with his girlfriend, or talk to her, but work demands all of his time and attention. He calls her as soon as he can, and this turns out to be Wednesday.

Since the woman isn't aware of how her boyfriend is feeling, as the week progresses, she isn't confident about the relationship. She is worried and concerned. When he does call, she tends to be irritated and unsettled. She feels the burning desire to ask him the three questions he fears most of all: "What's wrong?" "Can we talk about the relationship?" and "Where is our relationship going?"

This is extremely frustrating to a man. In his mind, everything is going well. As he sees it, he and his girlfriend are so comfortable that their relationship is basically on cruise control. Sure, he knows he's committed and monogamous, but he has never had to face that or say it out loud—it just kind of evolved that way. He is relaxing and enjoying the ride. In our scenario, the woman has dragged the man out of his comfort zone by bringing up their relationship as a topic for concerned, serious discussion.

We can grasp that a woman can become insecure because she isn't getting what she wants from her man—constant reassurance that he is committed. From our perspective, it seems she just doesn't understand him. She is unable to read the signals that he is sending. If she could, she would see that not only is everything going just fine but that her boyfriend is well on his way to the "commitment to engagement stage."

But that can change so quickly. With one question from his girlfriend, the man is reminded that, yes, he is in a committed monogamous relationship. This is like a bomb going off right in front of his face. He then realizes that he has to discuss the status of the relationship. He panics and gets defensive. Immediately, he begins to feel as if he is doing something wrong or that he isn't doing enough to make his girlfriend happy. He starts to feel as though he'll never make her happy. Then he comes to the question you never want him to ask himself—why am I committing to this dissatisfied woman who makes me feel bad and how could I even consider marrying her?

This tremendous snowball of negative thought builds in seconds. It's frightening but true. It might explain that change in your boyfriend's tone of voice when you bring up questions about the relationship. We don't mean to scare you with this, we are just being truthful about what goes through a guy's head when the commitment discussion is forced upon him.

A Strategy That Works

So what works? you might ask. We'll use Brad as an example. His relationship with his wife started out with casual dating, as most relationships do. With her good looks, intelligence, charm, and understanding, Cheryl was in Brad's "wife potential" category right from the beginning. As the relationship progressed, Brad and Cheryl found that they spent more and more time together. Soon they were with each other most weekend days as well as nights. As a matter of fact, this relationship started to get more and more serious during the summer, traditionally a time Brad dedicated to meeting and dating many women. Cheryl became central in Brad's life. Brad found in Cheryl that something special he had a hard time defining and she also knew how to nurture her Mr. Right.

As the summer months blew by, Brad continued his relationship with Cheryl. They gently progressed to a higher plane, reaching the "commitment to monogamy" level without Brad ever realizing what was happening. The fact that Brad wasn't sidetracked by bikini season just goes to prove that there really isn't a "right time" for a relationship to work. When the right woman walks into a man's life, he is ready. Any woman can maximize her chances with Mr. Right by understanding how to let the relationship unfold.

Fortunately, Cheryl somehow knew this. She did not pressure Brad about where the relationship was going. She did not mention the word commitment. She just enjoyed his company and the increasing amount of time she and Brad spent together. One day, Brad realized that he was in a committed, monogamous relationship that had evolved over time. He never made a conscious decision to be committed, nor did he ever discuss the issue of monogamy with Cheryl. He just "became committed." Cheryl was able to read Brad's actions and understand that he was monogamous.

This is really the way a man wants it. No relationship talk, no reminders that he can't be with any other women, no pressure. One day he realizes he is spending all of his time with a beautiful woman who makes him feel good and that it has been a while since he's dated others. He thinks that he could be very happy if the rest of his days were spent just as he has been spending them—with her. If you ask him later what happened, he'll probably say that he just found himself committed to her. He didn't plan it that way, it just sort of—happened.

So, if you want to keep your man happy and move him toward commitment, take a note from Cheryl's book. Maximize your chances with a professional man in these ways:

• Don't push him. Relax and enjoy the dating process. Take time to get to know one another during the first year of dating.

• Don't talk about the relationship every chance you get. Instead try to be sensitive to his actions and be confident that he is showing you how he feels by spending more time with you.

• Never bring up the M-word—Marriage—within the first year of dating.

8

—

How to Get Mr. Right to Pop the Question

Men and commitment. These two words have frustrated millions of women for thousands of years. Our women friends have told us that they are continually confused about how men view commitment. "Why are all men afraid of commitment?" is a question many women ask while they are in the dating scene. When women become involved in relationships, they often ask, "Why won't my man commit?" As these relationships progress, the question then becomes, "Will my man ever commit?" If these men still haven't committed, women take a more active stance and ask, "How can I get him to commit?" Unfortunately, when women try to force men to commit, the relationship fails and the question becomes, once again, "Why are all men afraid of commitment?" Many times this becomes a never-ending cycle of "noncommitment."

We sympathize with women when we hear the classic story of how the relationship is going so well . . . except there's no engagement ring or even talk of engagement. In this chapter, we will answer the questions that keep coming up in this "noncommitment" cycle. We will talk about why it takes men longer to commit than women would like. We will also reveal what goes through a man's mind when he thinks he has found Ms. Right. We will discuss what makes a man say, "I cannot live without this woman" and "I am ready to commit to her." Finally we will give our formula for how you can get your man to give you the engagement ring and ask you, "Will you marry me?"

The Slow Cautious Path to Finding Ms. Right

One definite fact that women need to know is that all men want to settle down and be in committed relationships eventually. The tall task a woman is faced with is to make her man realize that.

In our first book, *What Men Want,* we explained how men place women into two distinct categories, "good for now" girl or "wife potential." A man makes this distinction early on in the relationship, possibly even during the first encounter. For a man to consider becoming engaged to a woman, she must be in the "wife potential" category. Unfortunately, if a woman is in the "good for now" girl category there's no chance that a man will ever marry that woman.

A "marriage material" girl or woman with "wife potential" is the type of woman a man can see himself committing to one day in the future. She is the kind of woman he is proud to be around. He will open up his life to her. He will introduce her to his family, talk about her at work, and bring her to important business and social functions. He will be interested in her life. He will ask about her day at work, about her family, and about the important events in her life. Being in his "wife potential" category *does not guarantee* that you will become his wife. It simply means that you have the potential.

You may be asking yourself, "Why does it take so long for a man to realize that I am the woman of his dreams?" Once a man knows that he has found a "marriage material" girl a slow transition begins to take place. During this transition period, a man is taking in a lot of information about his potential wife. Every day, every hour, and every minute he is learning more and more about her. He is continually reevaluating her and what she does to see if she is the woman who will eventually be his wife.

What happens in a man's mind during this period? Well, he slowly begins to "allow" small thoughts of marriage to enter his mind. He thinks of his girlfriend and contemplates being married to her. What would it be like? At first, this is only a ten-second thought. It's a strange, uncomfortable thought, one that a man quickly forces out of his head. The next time this thought pops into his head, he thinks about it a little bit longer—maybe twenty seconds. Then thirty, forty, fifty seconds. He soon realizes these thoughts aren't so bad—in fact, they are good thoughts, thoughts that make him really happy. Slowly a man begins to warm up to the idea of getting married. He realizes he is actually capable of making a long-term commitment.

It's critical for a woman to understand that, for a man, the first thoughts of marriage are unnatural. A man is hardwired for variety when it comes to women. Darwin would back us up on this one—many offspring from many mates equals survival of the fittest. Today, men reinforce in each other the fact that these early thoughts of marriage are dangerous. For example, when a man gets engaged, his friends tease him. "Are you crazy?" they ask him. This reinforcement is pretty powerful and creates tension for men. Thoughts of marriage introduce an internal conflict in the man's mind. It takes the right woman to overcome this conflict.

The transition from a staunchly noncommitted frame of mind to one that is open to the thought of commitment is slow, because a man wants to make absolutely sure that the woman he has his eye on is The One. Making the decision to commit to marrying a woman is one of the most important decisions a man will ever make in his life. It can enhance his life tremendously if he makes the right decision, or it can make his life a living hell if he makes the wrong decision. Believe it or not, men do view marriage as an important, holy, and sanctifying experience, and they also know that it will affect every aspect of their lives. It will affect their work, their relationships with their friends, and their relationships with their families. Therefore a man is going to think long and hard before plunging into marriage. A misstep here could turn a man's whole life upside down and he knows it. In a man's mind, marrying the wrong woman could ruin his professional life, a life that took him many years of hard work to create successfully. As we mentioned earlier, all men do want to settle down and get married, but they will be very careful about whom they select and they will usually take their time moving a relationship with her toward commitment.

Relationship Coma—How to Prevent It

There is the danger of a man moving too slowly toward commitment. If a man is in a relationship with a woman for too long before presenting the ring, he slips into a "relationship coma." A man in this state has relaxed in the uncommitted status quo and, in effect, become stuck there.

It should not take a man more than three years to figure out if he wants to marry you. That's two years dating and one year living together. We strongly believe three years is the absolute outside deadline you should accept for a man to pop the question to you. If he has not committed to engagement by that point, then he never will. Thankfully for women, even men slow to commit don't take longer than five years from the first date to the walk down the aisle with Ms. Right (Marriage = two years dating + one year living together + two years of engagement). The key to preventing relationship coma is to bring up the topic of marriage, *but only at the appropriate time and in the appropriate way.*

Many women have scared off great guys and potential husbands by initiating the marriage conversation too soon. If a man hears this conversation prematurely in the relationship, he will think that his girlfriend is too pushy and that all she thinks about is marriage. In his mind, he is thinking, I am still trying to get to know her. How can she want to marry so soon in the relationship? She must only want a ring.

When Is the Appropriate Time to Bring Up the M-Word?

If your man has not initiated the marriage conversation by your one-year anniversary (which is most likely the case), then you should bring it up. Most men are thinking about marrying the woman they have dated for one year. They may not be ready to get married, but usually the thought has crossed their minds.

The next key consideration in discussing marriage with

your man is the manner in which you do it. Your girlfriends or even mothers may have told you "Why would he buy the cow if he is getting the milk for free?" We are astounded by how women, even sweet, dainty grandmothers, will refer to your relationship as a farm animal. Regardless of how many times you have heard such comments, we think you should avoid any reference to these sayings when you first bring up the idea of marriage with your man. Also, do not introduce the topic of marriage when your boyfriend has been drinking; he will resent the conversation later. It's best to discuss this serious issue when you have his full—and sober—attention.

If you want to see your man head for the nearest exit, give him an ultimatum. The worst thing you can do is force your guy into a corner and tell him either to commit to marrying you or else. You will never force him to marry you. If he was thinking about marrying you, then he will instantly drop the idea completely. Men don't respond well to confrontation, especially in relationships. If you give him an ultimatum, he will think that you are trying to control him. No man wants his future wife to threaten him—that only breeds ill will.

What Is the Appropriate Way to Bring Up the M-Word?

There's an art to bringing up the marriage conversation. If you master this art, then you will make your man want to marry you sooner. First, you should never actually use the word "marriage" as you introduce the marriage conversation. When a man hears that word for the first time in reference to a relationship he's in, he immediately goes into panic mode. He is stunned for the whole conversation, and he cannot think clearly. If you throw "marriage" onto the table, your guy will be on the defensive and will try to end the conversation.

The technique that will always work is to tell him how much you care about him, how he has made your life better, and how you enjoy spending time with him. If you initiate the conversation in that manner, your boyfriend is more at ease, because he knows that you truly care about him and that makes him feel good. On some level, your guy also knows that the "marriage conversation" is coming for the first time. If you ease into it, you will increase your chances of his being in the correct frame of mind to discuss it with you.

At this point, your man will either respond to your comments, telling you how he feels about you, or just smile and nod his head. If he doesn't respond verbally to your comments at this point, you should not worry. As everyone knows, men are poor emotional communicators who can't articulate their emotions as well as you can.

After your guy declares his feelings for you, or even if he sits there seemingly mute, you should then continue the conversation by telling him how compatible you think the two of you are and how you think you both could have a wonderful future together. He should respond at this point, but he may have a panicked expression, like a deer caught in the headlights. If he still has not responded, then your secret weapon to get him to talk is one simple four-word question, "What do you think?" not "How do you feel?"

If he still does not respond or does not tell you that he sees a future with you, then he is not interested in marrying you and you should leave him. If your guy has given a positive response and has told you that he sees a future with you then—and only then—you can add, "When you say a future, do you mean marriage some day?" If he says yes or responds positively, then he has essentially told you that he wants to

marry you. Now you should *stop*. Do not push him any farther than this.

Many women feel the need to put time limits on the actual
act of getting married during or after this conversation. This
is a huge turnoff for a man. If he has told you that he loves
you, wants to be with you, and can envision marrying you,
then that is great news. You are in a loving relationship. You
should not jeopardize it by pushing him and nagging him
about getting married. As we said before, marriage is one of
the most important decisions a man will make. If he is forced
to make the decision before he is ready, then he will back out
quickly. *He will love you more and want to marry you sooner if
you don't give him ultimatums or pressure him into marriage.*

Your first conversation about marriage with Mr. Right would
be on the right track if it went something like this:

YOU: Honey, I have been thinking lately about how the
time we spend together means so much to me. I can't
remember when I've enjoyed getting to know someone so
much. Since we met a year ago my life has been wonderful
and my love for you has grown stronger with each day.

HIM: (nods and smiles, holds your hand but says nothing)

YOU: You are the only man I have ever been able to cook
with and I love that we both like to travel and read and
work on the apartment together. Of course, just relaxing
with you on the couch on a Friday is my favorite way to
end the work week. In fact, I can't imagine my future
without you.

HIM: (dazed) Uuuuum-hmmmmm.

YOU: What do you think?

HIM: Well, I have pictured my future with you, certainly.

YOU: Does that future include marriage one day?

HIM: Yes.

Remember, *stop right there*. You have accomplished the mission of this first conversation—to get your man to say out loud that he has pictured a future with you that includes marriage.

Finding Ms. Right Will Change a Man Forever

So, what goes through a man's mind when he thinks he has found Ms. Right? When a man meets Ms. Right, he goes through an emotional metamorphosis. All of a sudden he is always happy and is always having a good time. He is more productive at work, and he is more social around coworkers. He's thrilled to spend time with his "marriage material" girl. He enjoys going to work to provide for her. He even enjoys doing mundane chores with her because he is spending time with her. He doesn't want to go out drinking and partying with his friends as much. He wants to be with his girlfriend always. He can't imagine living without her.

He is happy because the relationship is providing some stability in his life. The dating scene can be fun, but it can take its toll on a professional man. As a man gets older and more serious about his career, having to date different women and go out night after night is stressful for him regardless of the sex he may be getting. Most professional men in the dating scene hope that they can meet Ms. Right so they can move toward a happy, committed relationship. A smart and ambitious man knows that the right stable relationship can take the edge off his hectic and stressful life.

How Is a Player Transformed into Committed Partner?

Brad is the perfect example of how a typical "player" can be changed into a committed boyfriend after meeting Ms. Right. Before Brad met Cheryl, he was the type of guy who would go out and try to meet a different girl every night. He would collect phone numbers and would enter them into his prized black book. At times, he would be dating up to six women at one time. Though it appeared from the outside that Brad was having a great time living the crazy bachelor life, on the inside he was always looking for that special someone, Ms. Right.

Deep down, Brad wanted stability in his life. When Brad started dating Cheryl, his life totally changed and reflected this. The metamorphosis was complete—he went from wild bachelor to caring boyfriend. He had had a few long-lasting relationships in the past, but inevitably his bachelor life always continued. It took finding Cheryl, Brad's Ms. Right, to make him really want to commit.

To Brad, Cheryl was different from any woman he had ever met before. There was and is no close second. She is different because she makes Brad feel at ease. Cheryl is always in a good mood and as Chris always says, "She makes everyone feel like they are in a good mood too." Since Cheryl grew up with two brothers, she understands that men like to watch sports, hang out with the guys, have big egos, and that their careers are extremely important. Cheryl doesn't try to redirect Brad's focus from his career. She knows that her support for his professional life makes him love her more. Cheryl also kept the pressure to be engaged off Brad as well. She never placed a time limit on the relationship. She always seemed to enjoy the time that she and Brad spent together in and of itself. Cheryl's behavior and actions, in turn, made Brad more devoted and, of course, more comfortable in their relationship, which allowed them to get closer and closer.

The same kind of realization that Ms. Right had arrived occurred when Rich first met Marla. He was immediately attracted to her and sensed it was more than Marla's beauty that drew him to her. After their first encounter, Rich knew right away that Marla had "wife potential." They dated for some time and Rich became attracted to Marla's sweet, caring, and loving personality. He loved her because of her intelligence, her sense of humor, her compassion for others, and her deep understanding of him. She was like no other woman he had ever met. Rich fell in love with Marla, because she had everything he was looking for in a woman.

What Happens When a Man Meets Ms. Right?

When a man meets his Ms. Right, he admires her appearance and how she carries herself. He will tell her how good she looks, but probably not as much as she would like. A man loves this woman for everything she is, not just because of her beauty. In fact, he knows that there are better- and worse-looking women out there, but that doesn't matter anymore. The whole package—intelligence, sense of humor, personality, style, spirit, sensuality, and more—makes a man crazy about his Ms. Right.

Upon finding this special woman, a man assumes a role in his future wife's life. His life begins to mesh with hers. His daily routine includes her. A man develops a trust and understanding that he would never have with a man and only rarely has with women. To her he confides some of his deepest secrets. He even starts to sound and act like her! He begins using some of her lingo and copies some of her mannerisms. He ultimately becomes less insecure about himself and the relationship. He wants to marry that special woman who makes him feel so relaxed, happy, and complete.

Rich's and Marla's lives have grown together over the years. Although they have different personalities, they think like each other and know what the other wants and needs. Marla is the sweet, gracious, and carefree one of the pair. Rich is the typical goal-oriented, competitive, workaholic, professional male. Even with their different personalities, Rich and Marla innately know when the other is feeling sad, happy, hungry, thirsty, tired, or even sexy. One knows when the other wants to be playful or serious. Rich's and Marla's daily routine includes each other from the time they wake up to the time they go to sleep. Over time, Rich and Marla have become one. Rich has been able to achieve this type of closeness only with Marla, his Ms. Right.

Men Are Afraid of Commitment Because . . .

We have talked about why all men want to commit and how happy and fulfilled they do feel when they finally meet Ms. Right. But what about that alter ego—that little voice in his head telling him to stay single forever? A man struggles between the thought of being in a fulfilling relationship and remaining single and independent. When Ms. Right comes along, she can always make him see that the committed loving relationship is the way to go.

So what fears does a man have when he is thinking about committing to a woman and ending his single life? He is primarily thinking that he will not sleep with another woman for the rest of his life. This thought petrifies him. It's going to take a very special person and some time to calm his fears. *A man has to come to the realization that the whole package of Ms. Right is much better than a bunch of nights with many Ms. Wrongs.*

Men may also struggle with the loss of freedom that single life provides. They fear that once they are engaged or married they will always have to "check-in" when they want to do something. They fear that they will be unable to spend time with their friends. They fear the responsibility of having to worry about and care for another human being.

Men also fear the possibility of getting divorced if their marriage does not work. A professional man knows that divorce adds another level of stress and complexity to his already demanding life. He knows that a divorce will adversely affect or even ruin his long-term financial plans. He will be very careful before making the decision to marry, because if things go bad, there can be tremendous consequences.

A very wealthy man may even follow up his proposal of marriage with a conversation regarding a prenuptial agreement, so be ready for this. You may think that the man who brings up this topic has only money on his mind and no love in his heart. This is an extreme position to take. When a man with considerable assets raises this issue he is not saying that he does not love you, only that the financial aspects of your relationship must be addressed before you are united in the eyes of the law. If you are firmly against signing a legal document outlining the fiscal aspects of a future separation, know that it may mean the end of your relationship. If you truly love your man and want the relationship to work out, then try to stay calm, hire a lawyer to advise you, and show good faith to your husband-to-be that you are optimistic about reaching a mutually satisfactory agreement. However, if your man springs the prenup on you just before you walk down the aisle or he's not open to having his lawyer and your lawyer negotiate the points of the agreement, then you may want to seriously reconsider marrying him (both you and he should have separate, professional legal counsel to address the details of the agreement and to reach an agreement that is fair to both parties).

On the other hand, should you be the one with the wealth who brings the prenuptial agreement to the table, listen to your man's concerns and be willing to negotiate a bit. You are well within your rights to protect your assets, so if your man flatly refuses to even discuss such a document, you may be better off without him. Whoever starts the conversation—you or your man—just be aware that prenups are increasingly common these days, especially when vast assets are at stake. Particularly if either you or your guy is extremely wealthy, the prenup is yet another issue that may arise— another consideration that he must take into account before popping the question.

A man has to struggle with all these things when he makes the decision to marry. This is why most men are afraid of commitment. This is also why most men can take years to decide if their girlfriend is Ms. Right. A man will definitely get the courage to ask, "Will you marry me?" if his Ms. Right can understand and calm his fears about marriage.

You Have the Power to Make Him Commit to Marriage

Women really do have the power to make a man commit to marriage. Women just need to understand and know how to deal with men better. So how can a woman calm her man's fears of commitment? Basically, if a woman can show Mr. Right that she and his life won't change drastically after engagement, he will come around and commit to marriage.

In a man's pessimistic mind, he thinks that after he commits to engagement, his life—as well as that of his Ms. Right—is going to change into some hell that in no way resembles their current life together. He thinks that as soon as he commits to engagement, his sweet, kindhearted girlfriend will become a six-foot-five-inch, three-hundred-pound control freak who will never let him go out or allow him to do anything he enjoys again. He thinks that the earth will shake, the seas will dry up, and the sky will fall after he asks for your hand in marriage.

Use the Engagement Formula

If you can calm his fears, then he's yours. We have devised a formula for engagement that will guarantee a marriage proposal from your man. The formula incorporates methods we know make men feel more comfortable with commitment and marriage. This formula works on men in all three career stages—the Not-Yet-Set Stage, the Transition Stage, and the Successful Stage. So read on:

ENGAGEMENT FORMULA = Ms. Right + Don't Push + Staying the Same + Understanding His Devotion to Work

As seen above, there are four key elements to this formula. The first thing that is absolutely necessary in this formula is that the woman be "Ms. Right." There must be the highest level of attraction, trust, and understanding for a woman to be considered a potential bride. Ms. Right status in itself does not guarantee that a man will commit to marriage. Ms. Right must also refrain from forcing her man into marriage. She must remain patient.

Essential for the move to engagement is that Ms. Right also continue to do "more of the same" things that got her into the Ms. Right category in the first place. Don't spend any time trying to transform yourself into someone—or something—else now. This will only scare your man away. Finally, one of the most important and poorly understood aspects about a man is how important his work is to him. Ms. Right must also "understand and respect his devotion to work."

If a woman can accomplish these four requirements of the Engagement Formula, then she will definitely receive the ring.

9

—

MOVING IN

One question that we've been asked again and again is "Is it okay to move in with a man before engagement?" In fact, we've been asked this question so many times we have decided to devote a whole chapter to it. We feel that moving in with your boyfriend is a very important step and a turning point in the relationship. Obviously religious and moral beliefs have to be taken into account, but if you and your man are comfortable with the thought of living together before marriage, then you should.

We definitely recommend that a woman live with her boyfriend before engagement for several reasons. The main reason is that it brings the relationship to another level that cannot be achieved any other way. We agree that if you don't move in together, the relationship can only go so far. No matter what anyone says, you cannot truly know a person unless you live with him or her. Living together forces you to learn almost everything about each other and, as a result, your relationship becomes stronger with each passing day.

No one is ever fully prepared for moving in with his or her significant other. You never took a class on how to go about this in school, and your parents never taught you about it. This is just one of those circumstances in which you'll have to dive in when you think the water looks safe. This is your chance to smooth out all the rough edges and bumps in the relationship before you make that final commitment to each other. It's better to find out sooner rather than later if you are incompatible when it comes to living together with your mate.

Moving in together is a learning period, or more like a crash course, on how to live with your romantic partner. You now have a chance to learn each other's routine, quirks, habits, and faults. A couple who lives together experiences how to handle compromise with one another on issues like who showers first, who cooks and does the dishes, who takes out the garbage, and who walks the dog. It is a very important stage in a relationship. That's not to say it is all work. There is a lot of fun and excitement that comes with moving in with a person you love. You can share more time with your guy and enjoy the new intimacy that cohabitation brings.

Before they got engaged, Rich moved in with Marla, and Brad moved in with Cheryl. Both Rich and Brad knew that they wanted to become engaged to their respective Ms. Rights. The next logical step in both of their minds was to move in with the women who make their lives so happy. Rich and Brad felt that moving in was the only way they could learn everything about their girlfriends. After they moved in, each felt that he had developed a stronger and closer bond with his Ms. Right. For each man, living together brought his relationship to new heights. They both feel they proposed sooner as a result of cohabitating.

"Free Milk?"

You may be thinking that old farm adage again: "Why would he buy the cow if he's getting the milk for free?" The truth is that moving in with a woman is a *huge* step for a professional man. It means that he is seriously thinking about engagement. He is also thinking that he will pop the question if living together goes well.

In reality, moving in with a woman complicates a man's life. When a man moves in with a woman, he sacrifices a lot. He has to change his comfortable routine. He essentially gives up any chance of dating other women. He throws his black book away. When a man makes the decision to move in with a woman, he gives up a huge chunk of his independence *just for her.* It's not about getting "milk for free." It's about taking the relationship to another level. A man will do this only if the woman in question is special enough for him to do so. Only a woman whom he would want to marry would qualify for such a drastic lifestyle change.

As we have mentioned in earlier pages, a woman's looks, intelligence, sexual spark, confidence, sense of humor, and other attributes come together to form the "marriage material" girl to whom we'd seriously commit. We know the woman with "wife potential" will excite us for far more than one night of sex. This is one of the reasons why we'll move in with her. When you and your professional man decide to live together you should feel confident that you are sexually attractive to him in a way that will last for more than just a few passionate years. He would not be moving along the road to commitment with you if this were not the case.

Don't worry too much that more predictable sex or sex just once a week will send your guy roaming just as the two of you become more committed. It's natural that those wild nights of sex with your guy taper off. Having sex with him in the office, on the lawn, in the cab, and in the swimming pool will most likely become history, too. Whereas sex once used to be the main course of our dating lives, in our committed relationships, sex seems more and more to take the role of a spicy side dish or weekly dessert. Sometimes, as crazy as this seems, we don't feel in the mood for that particular dish. It doesn't mean we love the women we are committed to any less, or that we are any less committed to them.

From all you've heard about our focus on sex, you may be asking what we are thinking when we are in love but do not want sex as frequently as before. Let us explain. We like to describe what we go through as a maturing process. As single guys, we enjoyed chasing women for sex. Sex with a new woman was extremely exciting—we'd do it, over and over and over again each night, nearly every night. As committed men, now we don't. When we are in a long-term relationship, we simply have more ways in which we find gratification with a woman. We spend less time having sex and more time talking or doing other activities we enjoy with her. We are more comfortable with all facets of ourselves with these women and, as a result, explore the many ways we can become completely fulfilled in our relationship that go well beyond sex. Moving in just gives us more options.

As a relationship moves beyond those first months or years of new love and passion, the frequency and excitement of the sex can wane. A man has heard about this from other guys or observed it in previous serious relationships he has been in himself. We're not saying he loves this or is extremely comfortable with it, we are just saying he knows it happens. We're not so sure that women understand this. The moral of this story is that a woman should not (or at least try not to) become insecure about herself or the relationship due to the decreased frequency with which she has sex with him. Like other transitions toward greater intimacy, moving in can be stressful at first for you and your Mr. Right. Don't add the unnecessary strain of your fears over decreased sex. It's probably unwarranted.

When the Anxiety Level Is Sky-high

A man is very anxious when he first moves in with a woman, especially if he has never lived with a girlfriend before. Remember, in his mind a man has given up a lot to live with his woman and he wants to make sure that this move is well worth it. He wants the relationship and his home life to progress smoothly in spite of the big changes cohabitation brings. So what are men thinking just after they move in with a woman? Initially a man's antennae are up, he is looking very closely to assure himself that everything is okay and his world has not been destroyed by this new roommate. He is looking to see if there are any major conflicts or big-time issues that arise between you and him in this new living situation.

A man struggles with the fact that he has lost some of his freedom and independence. This is a traumatic event for him. He now has to answer to someone twenty-four hours a day, seven days a week. He doesn't have that free time alone to do whatever he wants. He now knows that every time he makes plans it must be for two *and* he has to confirm with his girlfriend first. This can be a big adjustment for a man.

So, don't be surprised if your guy draws some lines and tells you not to step over them.

Yes, there are some things that a man won't give up even for Ms. Right. He will look to see how you respond to these nonnegotiables in order to determine if you are trying to control him. For example, your guy may want to reserve a night to go out with his friends. He may need to watch football on Sundays. He may need to go to the gym three nights a week. If you value your relationship, you will let him and even encourage him to continue to do some of these "guy things." If he sees that you don't have a problem with his taking time for himself, then he will be more comfortable with the idea of living together, and he will continue to feel closer and closer to you as your time under the same roof grows.

Beware of Moving In for Convenience and Forever

Never move in together with your boyfriend solely because of convenience and always have a discussion with him about how long you plan to live with him before you become engaged.

Moving in with each other should be a carefully planned process for both of you. If a man wants you to move in with him on a whim because the rent will be cheaper, or his lease is up, or some other reason that arises out of pure convenience—don't do it. Also, be wary of an invitation to move in early on in a relationship. The time to move in with a man is after you have spent at least one year dating and feel you are close to engagement. To move in under any other circumstance is a mistake, and the relationship is destined for failure. Both of you will regret it. If a man makes a snap judgment to move in with you, then he is doing it out of convenience for himself and he is using you. He will just as easily make a snap judgment to move out, break up, and never see you again.

Second, it's important to talk about how long you both plan to live together before engagement. We would like to reiterate here what we have said before: We feel that you should date someone for one to two years before moving in together. An engagement should come after no more than one year of living with each other. That's a maximum of three years preengagement dating. If you have been living with your boyfriend for two years, and you are not engaged, then it's definitely time to have a frank discussion with him and move on if he doesn't commit.

Though a year is the maximum amount of time you should live with your man before becoming engaged, it's still a big mistake to tell your guy early on that you are giving him a time limit. He will take this as an ultimatum and think you are trying to control him. Instead, take a casual "This is what I have in mind, what do you have in mind?" approach. Do this in a conversation in which you both air your feelings about the future before you pack and move in. Talk about the fact that you definitely see cohabitation as a step toward a closer, longer-term relationship with him. Ask him what he thinks about this. Lead him toward the view that moving in will be one more way to ensure a future both of you can look forward to and plan together.

You may want to direct your conversation as follows:

YOU: Sweetheart, I have something in mind that I thought we could discuss.

HIM: Yeah, what?

YOU: Well, I thought it would be exciting to talk about the possibility of living together. You know, we enjoy each other's company so much and moving in together would bring us even closer than we are now. Waking up next to you each morning would be a dream come true.

HIM: There is so much to consider, how should we work this out?

YOU: At least for now, we only have to consider how much we enjoy being together. Over the next few months we could look at the practical aspects one at a time. Rome wasn't built in a day. I'm just glad we can have this discussion and that you think this would be a good move for both of us.

HIM: We wouldn't have to pack bags to sleep over at each other's places anymore. Let's look at the paper Sunday and see what apartments are going for these days.

After you move in don't bring up future commitment right away. Let him get used to this new stage of your relationship first. Steer clear of the topic unless he introduces it. Enjoy daily life with Mr. Right and just keep the year time frame in the back of your head. If he doesn't bring up engagement by the end of your first year of living together, raise the question of marriage in a conversation like the one we suggested in the previous chapter (see pages 92–95).

Whether he says it or not, when a man makes the decision to move in with a woman, he knows that he has made an unspoken promise to advance the relationship to engagement. Usually, a guy pops the question within six to twelve months of living with the woman he sees as Ms. Right. Even men with intentions of further commitment sometimes do get into a comfortable zone when they are living with a woman. In this situation, a man is enjoying "getting the milk for free" and needs to be nudged forward. You have to confront your man if he lapses into the relationship coma. Remember, if he isn't willing *to* commit to marriage after one year of living together, he never will and you should move on. Date 1-2 yrs

Live ē 1 yr   12-16 mos

Help Him Deal with the Anxiety and the Ring Will Come Soon

If you do all you can to make this transition to cohabitation smooth and relatively stress free, your reward will be an engagement ring sooner rather than later. Here are some practical steps that can help you along the way.

The Test Phase

It's a good idea to have a test phase in which you both live together for a week or two before your official move-in date. This helps you and your guy get used to spending a lot more time together. It also minimizes some of the anxiety and shock that inevitably come with the eventual move-in. During this time, you can also get a good idea of some of his routines, and he can get used to yours so you can let them flow uninhibited when you are sharing the same place. Be aware that this test period is by no means similar to the actual move-in. It just makes the transition somewhat easier, because you have a better idea of each other's habits and schedules before they have to meet the mesh test.

Rich and Marla had such a test period. Marla moved into Rich's place before they moved into their new apartment together. Rich and Marla had spent hundreds of nights at each other's places, but they never lived together for more than five days. During this test period, Rich was able to learn and adjust to his new roommate's daily routine. He learned how to cope with Marla's morning rituals—which included hitting the snooze button for almost an hour, applying body lotion in a long, drawn-out, ritualistic fashion, and primping with a hair dryer and makeup for almost thirty minutes. He also learned that it was not a good idea to distract Marla during her morning rituals or before her morning coffee. This added a whole new dimension to Rich's morning he never anticipated—and he learned to respect and appreciate his girlfriend's daily rituals. Marla and Rich were also happy and relieved that their new place would have two bathrooms.

After this preliminary test run, Rich breathed a little easier, having got a good indication that he and Marla would be compatible living together. With some of his initial anxiety diminished, Rich looked forward a bit more to moving in with Marla.

Raise Practical Concerns Up Front

It's also a good idea to be very open and talk about all of the practical issues of moving in together before you sign a new lease. Take time to listen to each other and respect one another's personal habits, interests, and space. Come up with strategies in advance that will help you cut down on the friction your different ways of doing things could bring about. How you approach the morning bathroom schedule, telephone usage, eating habits, food preparation, cleaning duties, and other household chores should all be discussed before moving in together. Don't "try to work things out" as these issues present themselves. Talking about these and other aspects of everyday living up front will prevent spats that can put a strain on your relationship as you try to adjust to the new phase moving in represents.

Also, do what you can to let your guy take the lead on the logistics of the move. A man has a definite game plan in his head on how he wants moving day to go. Most likely he has mentally mapped out how the move should occur, what things he definitely wants to keep and where he wants to put certain items. His plan is very important to him. If you try to change his plan, he will think you are trying to control him. Try to let Mr. Right have his way on this day.

The Furniture Fuss *FRASIER*

Furniture is a big issue that comes up during the move. What furniture to take, what furniture to throw away, give away, or sell, and what new items to buy—it all has to be discussed. A man almost always has a special attachment to at least one piece of furniture. For Rich, it was his large sofa with built-in double reclining chairs. For Brad, it was his reclining black leather chair with matching footrest. It's crucial that a man is able to retain his favorite piece of furniture in the new living arrangement—even if you hate it and it's an eyesore in the new place.

This piece of furniture is a symbol of his manhood, and it cannot—and should not—be taken away from him. Don't worry, he'll eventually grow tired of it. During the move-in and the two-month transitional period, it's essential to make your man feel more at ease. So let him take the things he feels comfortable having around him when you move in together. Sure, Marla hated the large sofa and Cheryl hated the leather chair, but they both understood that these items made their boyfriends happy. We thank them for allowing us hang on to our "security furniture." Your man will be just as grateful to you if you do the same.

Money Matters

Finances are another big issue that needs to be worked out and discussed before you become roommates. Who will pay the rent? The utilities and the phone bills? Should you open a bank account together? A professional man will not want to combine bank accounts early on when living together. His reluctance on this point has to do with his need for some independence. We think it's a good idea to keep separate bank accounts while you are living together and then combine them after you become engaged.

If you are working, your man will most likely expect you to pay for some portion of the bills. If you are making a similar salary or more than he is, he will probably expect you to split the rent and any mutual household expenses. A man does respect a professional woman, but he might feel that he is being taken advantage of if the woman is making more money than he is and still leaves him to pay most of the bills. So, pitch in financially when you move in.

When Rich and Marla first moved in together, Rich was a resident and was not making much money. In fact, Marla's salary was almost twice what his was. Before they moved in, they discussed how they would pay the bills and rent. Rich was concerned because he knew that he would be struggling to support both of them with his salary. Marla did not want Rich to pay for all of the bills and rent. She wanted to pay for her share of all the finances. This gave Rich a sense of relief, because he knew that Marla was concerned about him and did not want to take advantage of him. They agreed to split expenses down the middle even though Marla was making a good deal more than Rich. This was what made him comfortable, and Marla knew that.

Everyone's situation is different financially, but a man likes to feel that he is in control. Anytime there is a public display of cash, let him be the one to handle matters. If you take the lead in these circumstances, you will steal your man's sense of himself as the provider and risk wounding his pride. You do not want this. He will feel silly and defensive and may become angry or resentful as a result. So, if you go shopping, go to the movies, or simply grab a coffee, let him be the one who pays on a regular basis. Sometimes, when you want to make a point of "treating" your man, you can pick up a bill—on his birthday, or when he gets a promotion and you are taking him out to celebrate, for example. In general, let him get the bill when you go out.

Whatever you do, avoid being nitpicky about money— especially in public. Instead, work out an agreement together beforehand (e.g., you pay for laundry, he pays for cleaning supplies, you pay for groceries, he pays for dinners out). If you're dating a guy who splits everything down to the penny, then we have one suggestion for you: run for the hills!

Cleaning Concerns

Most men hate to clean around the house, hate to do laundry, and hate to make runs to the dry cleaner's. As a bachelor, laundry is a necessity because a man needs clean clothing every day. So he goes to the cleaners' on a regular basis. All other cleaning chores may rarely get done when a man lives alone. After all, cleaning the bathroom never really *has to* be done, and dirty dishes can just be taken from the sink where he stores them and cleaned for reuse, according to many a solo guy.

When a man moves in with his girlfriend, it often takes some time for him to adopt new habits and raise his standards where cleaning is concerned. Be aware of this, and don't hassle your man too much about cleaning when you first live together. When a man washes his girlfriend's clothes or takes his girlfriend's clothes to the cleaners', he does, in fact, come to the realization that he has entered a new stage in his life. You want him to come to this realization slowly so that he doesn't panic. Performing these homemaking tasks too often early on can actually make your guy think twice about the benefits of living together with a woman or being married. Ease him into this important transition. Little by little, you will probably find that your guy is offering to help with chores around the house. Let him take these responsibilities at his own pace, knowing that as he does he will feel more comfortable with the idea of engagement and marriage.

For example, going to the cleaners' was normally a mundane activity for Brad when he was single. He usually scooped up his clothing and took it to the cleaners', handing it over to Tony when he got there, and going to work without a second thought. Then, Brad and Cheryl moved in together. When Brad first took Cheryl's pink skirt and flower-patterned blouse to the cleaners', along with his suits, he hesitated at the counter. Tony was giving Brad amused, questioning looks—as if to say, Are you getting serious or cross-dressing?—and Brad was thinking about what he was actually doing. Brad never imagined that he would be assisting a woman with her laundry. He then realized that he was really in love and in a relationship that would lead to marriage. At that moment, Brad could picture himself married and that made him feel good. A simple act—going to the cleaners'—actually created a life-altering moment for Brad when it came to increasing his commitment.

Dinner Duties

Another mundane task that can be an issue for those newly living together under the same roof is dinner. After a hard day at work, the last thing any man wants to do is cook dinner. He just doesn't have the energy or the desire. During his bachelor life, your man has probably either ordered in or has made those tasty microwave dinners for himself that take just minutes. For a man alone, eating is simply a necessity at the end of the day—he knows he has to refuel.

When a man lives with a woman the eating arrangements have to be worked out. Will they order in, will she cook (because he won't), or will they eat microwave dinners? For most men, any of these choices are acceptable if both you and he are working. He is happy as long as he doesn't have to cook dinner when he gets home. If you don't work, your guy would probably like you to prepare some home-cooked meals.

We urge you to take the steps we've just shared because your man will see the first two months of living together as a make-it or break-it point in your relationship. He also may be a bit difficult to take at this juncture since he feels the need to assert his power and reassure himself that he is still master of his universe. This is the transition period during which things can turn sour very quickly. In this phase, your man most likely will be defensive, protecting what he sees as his dwindling freedom. During the first two months you're under the same roof it's best if you comment on or interfere with his schedule and habits as little as possible. You should let him grumble, strut around, and gripe as he settles in and gets comfortable in his new living situation. Trust us, once he feels secure and realizes that he hasn't made a big mistake and once he sees having you around is a bonus rather than a restriction on his life, he'll relax and his mood will improve.

If you can be the laid back and confident one and hold tight for a few months you will be rewarded. If there are certain things your guy is doing you just can't live with, just try to bear them for this short time. They may very well disappear once he becomes comfortable with the new living situation. If they don't, then gradually see if you can move him, with sensitive and caring comments, toward compromise on key issues. You don't want your man to sense that there's a dramatic change in his life just after the move because if he does he may have second thoughts. If you set your rules out strictly and sternly, demanding that your Mr. Right do this and not do that right off the bat, he may get scared and jump ship.

Emergency Exit

Part of a man's overall moving-in agenda includes an emergency plan. He comes up with a Plan B in case things go bad, especially early on. You won't have to worry about where he'll stay if things don't work out in the first few weeks you are living together. You can bet that your man has a carefully constructed plan about where he will go, what he will bring, and how he will escape if your cohabitation is a catastrophe.

When Brad first moved in with Cheryl, he had such a plan. For the first two months he had a hidden duffel bag of clothes, a room reserved at the Hilton, a rolled-up stash of cash, the hotel phone number on speed dial, and a driver on call—all just in case living with Cheryl didn't go as planned.

We are obviously being a *little* facetious here, but all men do think about what might happen if living together does not go well. (You should make sure you have an escape route, too—just in case.) Most guys do have some loose idea about what they will do if things do not work out. Don't think a man does this because he thinks moving in with you will be a failure or because he wants to exercise Plan B. A man's planning for the worst case scenario just goes to show how nervous he can be and how big a step moving in with his girlfriend often is. He comes up with the escape hatch just to ease his fears.

Where to Live

We've just touched on some of the more important practical issues that have to be worked out when you are planning to live together. Before we leave this section, we should discuss the question of where you both move in. Your first place together with your guy has a big impact on him. The choices you have are living together at your place, his place, or moving into a brand-new apartment together.

He Comes to Your Place

We don't suggest that you have your man move into your place. If you must, you must, but it is not the optimal situation as far as a guy is concerned. When a man moves into his girlfriend's place, he loses some sense of his masculinity. He is now thrown into a very feminine environment, and he usually has to leave behind most of his macho furniture and totems—neon beer lights, lava lamps, wet bar, and other bachelor pad items. Also, a professional man may feel as if you are providing for him by having him move into your place, which will make him feel very uneasy. Even if he is paying half of the rent or more, his moving to your place symbolically represents your taking him in.

When the time came for them to move in together, Brad did move into Cheryl's place. He didn't want to do it, but his lease was running out and she had another year on her apartment's lease. Brad felt very uneasy about moving into Cheryl's space because of its particularly feminine feel. He also knew how Cheryl felt about his stuff (she hated it and thought it was ugly)—even though she was being good about letting him move his black leather reclining chair in with him. In the first weeks and months, Brad felt as if he were crashing at Cheryl's apartment—for a really long time. He just didn't feel at home. This increased Brad's wariness about the move and was part of what made him so attentive to his emergency plan, which he was ready to implement at a moment's notice.

Brad's and Cheryl's relationship and living situation succeeded, though, because Cheryl was sympathetic and took what measures she could to help make Brad feel that her place was now his place, too. She tempered her feminine decor with some of Brad's favorite pictures and gave his recliner a prime spot in the living room. In short, she compromised some of her aesthetic preferences to accommodate him. This allowed Brad to feel more comfortable with the move.

The moral of the story is that if your boyfriend is moving into your apartment, realize that it makes the move more stressful for him. In addition to the anxiety of living together, he will also be trying to feel like the man he is in a feminine environment while mourning the loss of some of his prized possessions. A man facing this situation also has to convince himself that living at what used to be just your place does not mean that you are providing for him.

So what can you do to ease this anxiety in your man? Try to make him feel like your apartment is now his apartment, too. Ask his opinion about the furniture placement and decorations. Let him know you're willing to make changes in order to make him feel more at home. Nine times out of ten your guy won't try to change anything, but the fact that you asked and cared about his feelings will make him more comfortable in his new home and bring him closer to you.

You should also try to be open to change. If your guy was able to part with some of his belongings, then you should be able to as well. If you can afford to, you may want to consider buying new furniture together. Selecting and purchasing a new couch, bedroom furniture, kitchen table, or other household item gives you the opportunity to make a joint decision and show him you care about his input. He will see that you understand and respect his tastes and feelings—and that the two of you are a team. These types of interactions will help you bond, appreciate one another, and create a home together.

Shortly after he moved into her place, Brad and Cheryl went out to pick out a new TV stand. They shopped around, visiting a number of places, but the experience of this was anything but painful. It was exciting and refreshing for Brad. Brad realized that Cheryl suggested they get a new piece of furniture together because she wanted him to feel comfortable. That caused Brad to feel really good about Cheryl—and himself. After they both decided on a stand they liked and brought it home, Brad was not as concerned about how his and Cheryl's tastes might clash now and in the future. He saw that they could agree on things they both liked and that Cheryl was open to that kind of cooperation.

The most important thing you can do to make your boyfriend feel at home in your place is small but very significant. Stop calling the apartment or house "yours" and start referring to it as "ours." This reference will ease your boyfriend's fears that your opinions, ideas, and thoughts have more clout than his when it comes to your home together. He will see that you consider your home his as well and that you both have an equal voice on all issues that arise there.

You Go to His Place

The second scenario is when you move in with your boyfriend. This may not be the best situation either. As you turn up at his door with a truckload of your stuff on moving day, your man may feel that you are mounting an invasion. It is a bit emasculating for him when prized possessions, such as the black leather furniture, the strobe light, and leopard skin rug, go and are replaced with something Martha Stewart would approve of. Even if you are nice and diplomatic about integrating your furnishings and belongings with his, he may feel as though he is being pushed aside as you take what used to be his territory for your own.

Your guy may also be having a tough time changing the way he thinks about his space now that you are moving in. It may be hard for you to think about, but his place has been the scene of many memories he has of wild parties, late evenings, and seductive episodes with other women. Most likely, he has spent years in his bachelor pad and is wrestling to transform his vision of it from dimly lit party spot for the guys and "good for now" girl sex haven into a cozy love nest for just the two of you. Your man also may be concerned about just what woman from his past might want to look him up and be able to find him here, at his old address. He most likely would never share these things with you, but they might be a few of the thoughts that would make him feel uneasy about you moving into his place.

If you do end up moving into his place, tread carefully when you first arrive. Ask him where he would like you to put your things. Confer with him on which of his items he might part with as you start clearing the way for your own. You might see how open he is to a total rearrangement of the main living space—he might find a new look will help him get those old drunken and lusty scenes out of his head. You may also want to discuss what stays and what goes, or how you might rearrange his apartment before moving day.

If a woman calls or turns up on the doorstep one day, and your boyfriend seems mortified, don't make the situation worse. Let him tell this old "good for now" girl about his new situation with you and then let the subject drop. Most likely your man will be as embarrassed as you were to see or hear from this woman. Be understanding. Don't bust his chops on this one.

The Best Option—A New Place for Both of You

We feel that the best option is to find a new place together. This is the optimal moving-in scenario, because the space will be new for both of you. You also will have a chance to share in the financial responsibility with a joint signing of a lease. (Just in case the worst does happen and one of you decides to move out, it is wise to find a place that either one of you would be able to afford rent on alone.) The couple who finds a brand-new place also has the unique opportunity to choose a space they both like and decorate it together. This gives them a chance to discuss many issues during the process. By moving into a brand-new space, you and your man will feel as if the new living arrangement heralds a fresh start for the relationship.

Rich and Marla chose to live in a new apartment. They

had talked about the possible options beforehand and were able to make their leases end at the same time and start apartment hunting together. Once they found a place they both loved, they planned how they'd use each room, and decorated together. They also discussed which items each of them would bring to the new apartment. They learned about compromise and about each other's tastes in a situation much less loaded than they would have faced had they been moving into apartments either of them were currently living in. Moving into a brand-new place subsequently made the first stage of living together very easy for Rich and Marla. The whole process brought them closer as a couple.

Give Him Space

After the initial moving in takes place, the key to success for living with a man is to let him have some space and time for himself. No matter what his living situation is with a woman, a man still has to feel that he can be left alone if he wants to be. He has to have the security to know that if he has had a bad day or if he has an important project at work, he can think or relax away from everyone—including you. This is especially true during the first two-month transition period of living together. If your man feels he can't get some space or free time for himself, he will seriously reconsider his living arrangements and your relationship together.

If you see that your boyfriend has a lot on his mind from work and wants to be alone, it's best just to let him be. He will be grateful for this. Inside, he will be reassured that you are not trying to control him and are considerate of his feelings. Being able to perceive when a man needs space—and giving it to him—is an essential quality that a man looks for in his wife.

Next Stop—Engagement

We hope that you recognize that living together can be the best experience in the world for a seriously involved couple. Living with you enables a man to learn more about you, to enjoy your company on a day-to-day basis, and to discover how truly special you are. Living together helps your guy get used to sharing everything—chores, families, friends, and most important, time—with you. There will be rough patches, but if all goes well, the two of you will bond in new ways that help reassure your guy that marriage would be a good thing for him.

For a man, moving in is a huge step toward commitment to marriage. It is probably the most important move he will make pre-engagement that will show you he considers you his potential wife.

If a man agrees to move in with you, he is actually telling you that he wants to marry you. Your man also needs to feel totally comfortable with the relationship before he makes his final decision. We hope the insights and tips we've shared in these pages will help you put your Mr. Right at ease as you move into the final rounds of commitment with him—engagement and marriage.

10

ENGAGEMENT

For a man, getting engaged is no small potatoes. It is much easier for a man to say that he is going to get engaged than actually to present his girlfriend with a diamond ring. Why is this? As we have explained, every step in this commitment process is monumental for a man. Each bit of progress in a serious relationship brings a man closer and closer to the woman he loves *and* to never dating or having sex with another woman again.

Doesn't our point of view shed some light on why guys you or your friends have dated have had such a difficult time committing? Remember how those men had trouble staying in a committed relationship with you even when it was going very, very smoothly? And how many times have you seen relationships end because he hasn't popped the question?

As a woman, you want to be in the position of having your man in the "not a matter of 'if' but 'when' " situation by this time. You have dated, you have lived together—now the time is approaching when your man should make his final move. He should want to get engaged to you, but he still needs to warm up to the idea.

Think about it this way. Marriage is a fire—the closer your man gets to the fire the warmer and more comfortable he becomes, but getting close to a fire causes apprehension, too. Your man is thinking, I could really get burned here. What if I regret never having the chance to be with another woman again? What if she says, "No"? This is what men are experiencing as the relationship develops. We know we love this woman. We know that she is the best woman we have ever been with. We know that *eventually* we want to marry her and have a family with her. We just need a little longer to gather the courage to make that final move.

Brad thinks back to when he was considering the big step of getting engaged. He'd been living with Cheryl for about a year and the thought of engagement was popping up in his head more and more often. He was facing all the typical questions. Things were so good as they were, why change? Why should he have to look for a ring? Think about engagement? Family visits? Planning a wedding? Registering for gifts? He was in no mood to begin this whirlwind.

We know that once we purchase the most expensive gift we'll probably ever buy in our lives—the ring—the clock begins to tick. Tick-tock, tick-tock—time runs against us as that diamond weighs heavy in our pockets. The next thing we know—we are married. There's no stopping this clock. Why set the timer for the countdown if we don't have to?

To a man engagement is the most wonderful yet the most

anxiety-provoking point of his personal life. He knows that as soon as he asks you to be his wife the flood of social obligations will begin. The announcements, the guest lists, the invitations, the parties, the gifts, the wedding planning, and the honeymoon decisions are all going to be upon him, making the engagement period very time-consuming and stressful. With this in mind, a man will definitely not want to start this process while he is involved in a critical phase of his career.

Brad's friend, Erick, the chief executive officer of an Internet start-up company, was ready to propose to his girlfriend, Robin, a corporate lawyer. Around the time he decided he was ready for marriage, Erick was given the responsibility of hiring people for three major positions at work and preparing for the company's upcoming IPO. He knew that as soon as he popped the question, both his and his fiancée's lives would become even more hectic than they already were, given all of the wedding plans and family obligations that would arise.

As much as Erick wanted to ask Robin to marry him, he also knew that this was definitely *not* the right time in his life to propose. Erick was under tremendous pressure at work and he knew that adding the stress of wedding plans on top of that would be too much for him to cope with. He and Robin talked about getting engaged and Erick told her about his situation at the office. She understood and waited patiently as Erick became more settled. Erick's desire to marry Robin grew even stronger after they talked. It proved to Erick once again that in addition to her beauty, intelligence, sense of humor, and sweet personality, Robin truly cared about him and understood his devotion to work. He knew that Robin was the only woman for him.

Making the Decision to Pop the Question

Brad remembers distinctly his thoughts during this transitional period. He knew that he wanted to get engaged and marry Cheryl. The time felt right. His career was beginning to settle down. He had been in private practice in his own law firm for a while and felt secure. Feeling that life requires some definitive action, he decided to move ahead. He knew that he wasn't going to get married without first reaching down inside himself and coming to grips with the many implications of marriage. He knew he was face to face with one of life's biggest decisions.

A man doesn't necessarily want to face this decision. He eventually addresses it because he knows he has to—if he wants Ms. Right and the life he has been envisioning with her for himself. To help make this decision he literally needs time just to sit and think. Brad did just that. He focused on the question of his future and pondered all of his options. He looked at the pros and cons of staying single and getting married. In the end, Brad became extremely excited about making a lifetime commitment to Cheryl, so much so that he made it his immediate business to purchase the engagement ring. He needed to get his finances together within the next couple of weeks, select the ring, and put the money on the table. He was ready to move ahead.

How do men come to this pivotal moment in their lives? How do you get your man to take that last and most important step? To answer this question you probably want to know what Brad was thinking during that pondering stage. Well, he thought about Cheryl of course. He thought how she had been so very supportive during so many transitions in his life. He realized that she never pressured him or placed self-imposed time limits on the process. Brad thought specifically of the promise he made Cheryl. He told her when they moved in together that he was very much in love with her, said that he wanted to marry her, and planned on doing so eventually. He thought back to the time when they were moving in together. He remembered how Cheryl's family had been very strongly opposed to the idea. Cheryl stood up for herself in the interest of their relationship and fought her family over the issue. Cheryl took a risk to be with him.

Brad recognized how well Cheryl treated him and how good she made him feel. And he remembered his promise to her. Cheryl knew not to push Brad into engagement. She knew that a man needs time to sort these things out. He owed it to her to propose, and he owed it to himself. He realized that proposing to Cheryl would be exciting and meaningful for their relationship.

Brad appreciated that Cheryl was so giving of her time and patience and never made an issue of timing. Furthermore, she allowed the relationship to take its course, progressing naturally. This caused Brad to feel one way and one way only: he wanted to marry Cheryl. After Brad had time to think about his relationship with Cheryl, the only thing Brad could think of was marrying her. He knew he wanted to do it. The little things that Cheryl did and didn't do caused Brad to trust, respect, and love her. Once he saw this, there was no reason not to marry Cheryl. By taking the right steps and letting your man come to these same conclusions, you can help him become excited about lifelong commitment and marriage.

Rich trod a similar path with Marla. The mutual promise that he would marry her and she would be patient until he was ready was evident with them as well. Marla had been patient despite the many naysayers who told her Rich would never pop the question.

What people didn't take into consideration was how honorable a professional man can be. Rich knew he would ask Marla to marry him, but he was waiting for the proper time in both their lives. When Marla and Rich began to live together, Rich didn't know where he would be accepted for his fellowship. The time came when he was accepted into a New York City hospital. He told Marla, wondering how she would react to this news, and found that she was just as excited as he was about the life they could have together in New York. At this point, Rich felt he had at least some direction for the immediate future. He knew it was the proper time to ask Marla to marry him.

Should a Woman Consider Popping the Question?

We're sometimes asked how we feel about women proposing to men. We say wait for the next millennium for this to be acceptable to men. We may have come a long way, but men have not come far enough to feel comfortable with a woman popping the question. Yes, a woman can ask a man out for date. Yes, a woman can call a man. Yes, she can ask for his phone number or e-mail address. And, yes, she can offer to pay for dinner on a date on occasion. But, no, she can't ask a man to marry her. Not if she wants him to say "yes." It just doesn't work.

A guy can't get married that way. He wants to be in the driver's seat when it comes to the life decisions he makes, and marriage is certainly a life decision. When a woman asks a man to marry her, he feels castrated—she's taken an important moment of honor and control away from him. In asking a man to marry her, she also is bound to catch him off guard. In the best cases—when men ask women to marry them— they feel inexperienced and inept. When it comes to propos- ing marriage, we men are novices. Professional men hate to be beginners in anything. We pride ourselves on our ability to achieve, to get ahead, and to prosper. If you beat us to the punch on the proposal, we'll not only be stunned, we'll be defensive, angry, and insulted. Do you think we'd say yes in such a state? We wouldn't. Do you think we would ask you after you had asked us? We wouldn't. If you're thinking about proposing to your man—don't.

Engagement Practicalities

So, your man finally decides it's the proper time to propose. There are many practical issues that men need to address. But what does he actually do next?

Buying the Ring

Purchasing the ring is the first—and the most important— practical step a man takes toward getting engaged. How can a couple get engaged without a diamond, right? *Wrong!* That was a trick question. A man wants to know that, with or without a diamond, the love of his life will still want to marry him. The reason we think this way is that men get engaged and married without being wooed by some expen- sive gift. *We do it for free!* With this in mind, we think you should, too.

But, of course, your professional man will want to adorn your third finger with the beautiful ring of your dreams. But how are we supposed to know what to do, where to go, and whom to speak with about buying this important symbol of commitment? The problem is that by the time men reach this stage in a committed relationship they have heard all the horror stories about purchasing rings—whether it's the traditional diamond ring or, for the more adventurous, a ring made with another stone or combination of stones. We've heard about guys getting taken for heavy prices and receiving fake or poor-quality stones. We don't want to be that guy. As a result, it can take quite a bit of time and energy for a man to find and buy the ring he needs to actually pop the question.

In our experience, the woman who dates the professional man usually does want a diamond, but this is not always the case. Rick had been dating Sarah for three years when they talked seriously about marriage. Sarah told Rick she would love to marry him but that she didn't want a ring. Sarah never wore jewelry and felt an expensive engagement ring was a waste of money. Instead, she and Rick decided to invest in a two-month hiking trip in Brazil. They would get married in a simple ceremony there and then canoe down the Amazon. Rick was thrilled and we thought he was a lucky dog!

Don, another friend of ours, found out that his soon-to-be fiancée, Amy, didn't want a diamond ring either. Amy's father had proposed to her mother with a ruby ring and she wanted to keep the tradition alive, according to Amy's best friend, whom Don had called hoping for just this kind of specific information. He wanted to surprise Amy with a ring, but he also wanted to be sure that he got Amy a ring she would love. When Don presented her with the ring, Amy was touched to see that he'd gone to the trouble of discovering exactly what she wanted. Three years after their wedding, Amy still tells the story of Don's sleuthing and her best friend's ability to keep his proposal a secret.

There is certainly more than one way to get engaged. If

you and your boyfriend have discussed the topic of marriage, be sure he knows any strong feelings you have about the engagement process or ring, especially if it would make his duties in this area simpler. When we think of engagement, we tend to think of the most common situation—a surprise proposal with a diamond ring. Most guys we know do the same. But, some women don't want a ring, don't want a diamond ring, don't want to be surprised, or would prefer to be proposed to first and then share the financial investment of a ring together with their fiancé after he has popped the question. To avoid any misunderstandings and hurt feelings at this highly charged moment in your relationship, communicate with your man.

In Search of the Diamond

If your man is ready to invest in the diamond engagement ring and you haven't steered him toward another alternative, he must research where to go to find a good one. Hopefully, a recently engaged friend or family member will be able to advise him on this matter. The next thing he worries about is the size and style of the diamond. What do we know about these things? In a jewelry store, guys are like fish out of water. Brad had never bought a diamond before he bought one for Cheryl. So what did he do?

To begin with, Brad took Cheryl to a popular jewelry store in Manhattan. As they were strolling down Fifth Avenue on a Saturday, Brad maneuvered Cheryl toward the main entrance of Tiffany's. This was a full six months before Brad actually asked Cheryl to marry him and they got engaged. As they entered the store, Brad almost lost Cheryl in the crowd. She was headed toward the men's accessories department thinking that Brad was interested in another set of cuff links. Brad dodged around the glass cases to catch up with Cheryl and direct her to the engagement ring section, much to Cheryl's surprise. They approached the counter and that was the beginning of Brad's diamond education—and search for the right ring.

Let us tell you the significance of this process to a man. After a guy has decided that you would be willing to marry him without a diamond, he needs you to help him find a diamond. What we mean is that your guy wants to buy the right ring and needs your input. However, he doesn't want to ruin the surprise completely. So, usually a man will take a woman to a jewelry store or two and get her opinion on the diamond's shape and the setting. He will take care of ordering the diamond and the setting and picking the ring up. He will choose a time to pop the question and present the diamond that he hopes will be a surprise.

Keep in mind that you can ruin the entire experience and derail your relationship even at this stage by being too demanding. We recommend that you be fairly nonchalant about the procedure of diamond selection. Gently lead your man by asking him what he likes for you and then agree with him when he reaches the diamond (or other stone or combination of stones) that you find most appealing in shape and setting.

The worst thing a woman can do is dictate to a man that she has certain qualifications when it comes to ring size and other specifications. Chris had dated a woman fairly seriously when they began talking about a mutual friend's recent engagement. She mentioned their friend's ring. Chris noted that it was beautiful when she chimed in on how small the diamond was and that the guy should have spent more money on it if he "loved" her so much. Oh boy, did Chris lose that woman's phone number in a hurry!

In a similar case of don't-let-this-happen-to-you-if-you-ever-want-to-get-married, a mutual friend of ours was dating a woman who would often be heard telling her friends the exact specifications of the diamond she expected when she got engaged. It was disgusting to hear the woman recite "three to four carats, E color, and no worse than VVS-2." We found it sickening. We know for a fact that she is still out there seeking her special man.

Our advice? Be excited and show you are touched that your man is including you in the selection of the diamond that will move your relationship to the next level. Be non-chalant about the diamond itself. Ask your man's advice and try on rings that he suggests. This is a delicate situa-tion. For a man, choosing a diamond with the woman he wants to marry is much like having sex for the first time with a woman whom he loves. He doesn't want this woman to seem as if she has been with hundreds of men, directing him with specific instructions on what to do, and where to touch. He likes to see her flushed with excite-ment, looking into his eyes, rather than at what he has to offer in terms of physical accoutrements. Being a little naive is a good thing sometimes. Let your man take the lead. Give him the opportunity to feel good about his choice and taste. Remember an engagement ring is his gift to you and he has to see you with it on for the rest of your lives.

However, this is your chance to get what you want. Don't pass up the opportunity. Men do expect some guidance here—otherwise, why would they be taking you along to Tiffany's? Be subtle about your opinions and try to come to a decision together. Brad had Cheryl try on a variety of diamond cuts and they both came to the conclusion that a round diamond was the prettiest for her. That shopping excursion was definitely a success.

Many men hesitate when faced with buying an engagement ring. A man realizes that an engagement ring is a symbol of his loving commitment to you and he wants to give you a beautiful piece of jewelry you'll love and he'll love seeing you wear. But, even so, who wants to part with two months' salary on something this small in size that has no obvious function? We all know that when it comes to diamonds, size and quality are directly related to the price. So why doesn't a man buy his best girl a diamond chip and call it a day? Here's the rub—perception plays as great a role in the man's mind as it does in the woman's when it comes to the diamond engagement ring. We know that, to some degree, this ring is a reflection of our financial success. We know that special woman in our lives will wear it for decades. Even though you have told him over and over that you will accept a half-carat diamond, your professional man still wants to buy you what he thinks you deserve—and that is the biggest diamond he can afford. But most men have a practical side that can make them hesitate in the face of spending two months' salary or more on a ring. You can understand this, can't you? Be patient. It just may take your guy some time to make the purchase.

This is another reason why a man's career stages connect up with the development of a serious relationship. Before a man buys a ring, he needs to feel that he is financially stable. He needs a nice salary to be able to buy a decent diamond without going into debt. When Brad went looking for a ring, he made sure he was financially stable. When he began the search for "the rock" it was a conscious decision based on financial calculations. It wasn't haphazard. He didn't just dig in to a treasure chest and pull out the perfect diamond. As a matter of fact, Brad often said to people after he and Cheryl were engaged, "Do you know how many criminals I had to defend to get the kind of money it took to buy that ring?" He was being funny, but, in reality, Brad's comment wasn't far from the truth.

We want to make sure you see this from our perspective. We are spending a hell of a lot of money on a very small object. We want you to be entirely blissfully happy. We also want you to glow and gush. If you haven't figured it out yet by reading this book, we'll say it again . . . men want to please women. Presenting a girlfriend with a diamond ring is a very high moment in a man's life. A man wants to see and be able to remember for years to come the joy he sees in his girl-friend's eyes when he asks her to accept the ring and marry him. Brad clearly remembers the happiness he saw in Cheryl when he presented her with the engagement ring. She beamed and welled up with tears. That made all he did to get the ring worth it to Brad.

Popping the Question

Your man has the ring. He purchased it from his mother's friend's nephew whose father-in-law is a jeweler. He seems to be a lot lighter on his feet. (He is a lot lighter, thousands of dollars lighter.) Anyway, your man has to think up a way to propose to you. Again, having low or no expectations is the best way to go here. Try not to put pressure on your guy for something incredibly original. If you are like Rich, simple is better. Brad felt the same way, too. Even so, they wanted their proposals to be the finest moments of Marla's and Cheryl's lives. As men, we don't need to hear from you how you expect that we are going to surprise and thrill you with our proposal of marriage. We already have this pressure—we impose it on ourselves.

We know we have to plan a special proposal. We wish we could avoid this and the pressure this places on us, but we know we can't. We are overpowered by what we feel to be the implied pressure coming from our women. Even if our girlfriends don't say a thing, we know that if there was ever a time for a man to be romantic, it is at proposal time. So we do our best. We order limos and make reservations at expensive restaurants. We chill champagne, we practice lines, we sweat over the perfect moment to ask the woman with "wife potential" if she will marry us. We hope our girlfriends will see how hard we are trying, even if everything doesn't go as planned, even if we can't get out the words we hoped to say. Even if nerves get the best of us, we hope the ring will speak for our love and devotion, in a way that we have a hard time expressing in words. We hope she will look into our eyes and say one word—"Yes."

Rich remembers how he got engaged. He remembers that it was an especially romantic moment. It lacked any element of surprise (Marla knew that Rich already purchased the ring), but this was not important to Marla. Rich proposed to Marla over a romantic dinner that included champagne and red roses and candlelight. He presented Marla with the ring after he told her how he felt about her and reflected on all the wonderful times they had spent together. Marla accepted Rich's proposal with a smile he won't soon forget.

Brad used the element of surprise for his proposal. His plan was not all that intricate or original, but it was a surprise, and Cheryl loved it. It went like this. At the end of a typical workday, Brad called Cheryl at her office and told her that he was picking her up at work because he had just finished a meeting in the neighborhood. Cheryl didn't know that Brad had chosen this day to propose. She got his call and agreed to meet him downstairs, thinking they would go home and order in Chinese.

Cheryl went downstairs to find Brad seated in the back of a white stretch limo. She found this to be a bit strange but happily jumped in, thinking that the car service had sent Brad a limo only because none of the other regular cars were available. As soon as Cheryl sat down and pulled the door closed, Brad presented her with the ring and asked her to marry him. The proposal was quick and to the point. Cheryl was ecstatic. Brad was happy to see her so happy and excited. The limo combined with the element of surprise compensated for Brad's lack of romantic ability.

We do have some friends whose proposals have been a bit more elaborate than ours were. Their stories are fun to tell and will show you what some men will do to be sure the moment they pop the question is a very memorable one.

About six years ago our friend Brenda told us she was going to Disney World for a week with her boyfriend Jack. When she and Jack returned home to Chicago she didn't have a tan, but she did have a ring and a great engagement story. As it turned out, Jack told Brenda he was taking her to Disney, but didn't say which one. Brenda assumed they were headed to the Florida theme park and Jack let her go on believing that. When they arrived at O'Hare airport, Brenda made a beeline for the domestic counter while Jack walked toward the international flight desk. When Brenda came over to tell her boyfriend he was on the wrong line, he said that this was the right line if you were going to Disney—in France! Brenda was thrilled. She loved Jack's surprise and didn't know that this was only half of it. On their second night in Paris, Jack proposed to Brenda over dinner in a restaurant on the Champs-Élysées. Brenda burst into tears and said, "Yes, yes, yes!" She told us that she couldn't have imagined a better proposal. She and Jack set the wedding date for a year later. They've been married five years now and are expecting their second child.

No one can compete with Jack's approach, but Jason comes closest. Jason, a friend who lives in Florida, told his girlfriend of two and a half years that he wanted to take her out for her birthday. He said he had made a table reservation at the Delano Hotel in South Beach for the upcoming Friday night. What he didn't tell Cindy was that he also made a room reservation upstairs. He waited until after he had paid the dinner check to share that with her. Cindy was delighted at the romantic turn the evening had taken. Jason usually wasn't the one to plan such things. You can imagine Cindy's surprise when she opened the door to their room to see a vase of long-stemmed red roses, champagne chilling in an ice bucket, and a silver platter of strawberries. Jason closed the door, got down on one knee, and asked Cindy to marry him. With a tearful kiss, she accepted the ring he presented. At the wedding, Cindy told us that Jason had made every birthday memorable, but that the one on which he proposed to her took the cake.

So what can you do to make the question-popping ceremony a comfortable experience for your man? Make him feel great about the manner in which he chooses to propose. Keep in mind that his intention is to make this a memorable experience for you. He may simply be limited in his romantic flair. Any disappointment he senses from you would be devastating for him at this special moment. Remember that your reasonable expectations will make it easier for Mr. Right to propose. If he knows that you "expect" certain things, well, you'll be waiting to get engaged for a long time as he rallies his forces to meet your demands. If your expectations are too great, you may wait forever for a proposal that never comes.

The Ring's Not Your Thing?

Women always seem to ask us what they should do in the event they do not like the ring their men buy and present to them with the proposal of marriage. If you wanted an emerald cut and he gave you a pear-shaped diamond, should you say something or not? We recommend that you say nothing. Even if this ring is the ugliest piece of jewelry you've ever seen—say nothing. Yes, we mean nothing. That is, of course, if you still want to get engaged. Accept the ring with a smile and wear it proudly. If you make any indication you are anything short of ecstatic, your man will be severely disappointed, so much so that he may not have the desire to follow through with the wedding. Can you blame him? Just think what he's gone through to get to this point. Remember, too, you are marrying the man, not the ring.

Once you are married and comfortable, you might gently suggest that you might be happier with a different ring. But, who knows, you may have grown to love it.

Vacation Required

After the proposal comes the whirlwind of excited families and friends offering congratulations and asking questions about the wedding that has to be planned. A date must be set, and preparations must be made for the big day! This is torture for most men. All we want to do is relax—and try to recover from the monumental decision, the financial drain, and the stress becoming engaged has put on us.

Usually, we have no chance for a break. This is when our fiancée wants to tell the world about our engagement and take us along for the ride. We believe that the man deserves a vacation immediately after the proposal. No dinners with family, no parties with friends, no being congratulated by people he barely knows. All he wants is a bit of peace. But nope—he doesn't get it. You must try to understand how your man feels at this point. By revealing what your guy has been through in this book, we hope you will see that he needs time to recover.

Excited as you may be, do your best to recognize that your man is mentally exhausted after he proposes. Give him some time to revive himself and reflect on the situation and he'll love you all the more. He wants to be able to think about what he has done. He also wants to see you happy with him alone. Don't drag him out and show him off to all your friends and family immediately. Instead, why don't you try to slip away for a romantic weekend just with him? If you could plan and orchestrate such a getaway, your man would be so grateful. At this stage, he wants you (and only you—not friends, not family—not wedding planners) by his side. After all, it's you he loves and wants to be with. If you don't acknowledge what he has already done and show your appreciation by giving him time to rest, if you become too demanding at this point, your man may rethink his proposal. You wouldn't want that.

The Wedding Planning Process

Planning for a wedding is no small undertaking, and the professional man knows this. Furthermore, your man is not exactly thrilled at the notion of a year of wedding planning taking up all your free time as a couple. As a matter of fact, if your guy is anything like us, he probably wants to know that you will not be relying on him for all that is required to put together the biggest party of your collective life.

In order for you to understand this, we will offer an example. At the hospital where he did his residency, Rich met Bill, who had recently started building a practice in sports medicine and just got engaged. Bill had proposed to Debra, an interior decorator he had been dating since he started medical school. Before they got engaged, Bill made it clear to her that he wanted to marry her in the kind of wedding she had always dreamed of, but he would not play an active role in the day-to-day planning of it. Debra acknowledged what Bill had to say. She assured him that he would not be bothered with any details. She told him that her mother and sister would be able to help her when she needed assistance. She made good on her promise—Bill was left to focus on work and his career. Debra didn't force him to listen to one band, speak to one photographer, sample one food tray, or pick one flower or wedding invitation style. Debra saw to all of the details. All Bill had to do was turn up on their wedding day. It was obvious from Debra's response that she relished the opportunity to work on this project independently. When this happened, Bill knew that he had, indeed, chosen the right woman for him.

We comprehend the importance of the wedding and what goes along with it. In no way are we belittling the experience and excitement of the big day. In no way are we looking to take the excitement away from our wives-to-be or our loved ones. However, men like us prefer to play a secondary role in the planning process.

When we decide to marry you, whether you know it or not, we have already judged you to be a good "wedding maker." What we mean is simply that we like your taste and what you represent. We are sure that you will make terrific decisions and have our best interests in mind for the special day we will share. If we were not sure of this, we could not marry you. When we ask you to marry us, we are confident that you are truly our better half and we respect you and depend on you to be just that. Take our word when we say that we trust you with all the details. We know we can count on you to create a memorable and beautiful wedding day at which we will proud and honored to appear as the groom.

On the other hand, we are cognizant of the fact that there are many, many decisions to make and, of course, no human can make these all alone. We know we'll have to make it known whom we'd like to invite and what we'd like to wear. That is why we will step forward and offer opinions on issues you bring to our attention. But try to be considerate and thoughtful about the questions you raise to us. As you know, we are busy working and saving for that honeymoon and the house that we've been talking about buying after the wedding. And, please, don't mistake our lack of enthusiasm in dealing with wedding details as a diminishing desire to marry you. Nothing could be farther from the truth. We want to marry you and spend the rest of our lives with you. We will love you even more if you take over the wedding planning and leave us in relative peace throughout the engagement. After all, the wedding's really for the bride. The tune played at almost every wedding we've ever attended is "Here Comes the Bride . . ." We do not know of a song that cele-

brates the groom. The bride is everything. Everyone loves to
see how beautiful the bride is. We surely do, and we want
you to have the day you want and deserve.

As long as we are being honest here, all the attention going
to the bride is a bit hard for men to swallow. When you do
involve your man in the wedding details he must be involved
in to make your day a success, make him feel like the smart
and helpful guy that he is, even if no one else around you
does. Your man will appreciate you once again for this
thoughtfulness and understanding.

For example, on a visit you and your man make to choose
the catering hall, the caterer will direct all questions toward
you. He'll remind you that it is *your* special day. Your man
will think (for one small second) "What about me?" Whenever possible, make it clear to people around you that
although you are making most of the decisions, this day is
just as important to your man as it is to you. He should be
addressed as a knowledgeable party with an opinion that
counts.

Brad remembers the wedding planning process clearly. He
was a little upset that the few times he did give his input on
the ceremony, it was ignored. One time this happened was
when Brad told Cheryl he didn't want them to do the corny
walk-in introduced by the D.J. as Mr. and Mrs. Bradley
Gerstman at the start of the reception while everyone stared.
Brad was told that this happened to be Cheryl's favorite part
of the big day and he was asked if he wanted to stand in the
way of Cheryl's dream. Brad was hurt by this response. He
felt as though no one wanted to hear his input and stopped
giving it. As professional men, we are not often ignored.
We're used to making decisions—many times important
decisions that people respect. As the groom, we are treated

differently. People often don't acknowledge or respect what we say. Brad was annoyed by this reaction that people had toward him about his wedding.

Cheryl did what she could to soothe Brad's feelings and keep his opinions in mind. For instance, Brad was against having the three-hundred-plus-person affair she mentioned she would like. He didn't want to be the groom in a wedding attended by a crowd of guests who were strangers to him. For his wedding, he wanted only people who had a sincere desire to be there to be invited, for Brad could remember many times he had been asked to weddings he didn't want to attend. He didn't want the distant acquaintances who didn't really want to be there anyway to fill up his special day. Granted, this wasn't entirely accomplished, but the size of the wedding did not grow out of control. A small victory for Brad.

Planning a wedding is very stressful to a man who is used to controlling his own life and destiny. If the planning just included the woman he wanted to marry and himself, it would be a much easier situation to cope with. Inevitably, his mother-in-law-to-be immediately pops up onto the scene. Many times she runs the show, making the day more her own than her daughter's, the bride. This will take the pressure off the bride, but it does so with the possibility of adding a speed bump to your relationship with your man. Be aware that the choices made while planning a wedding can be very confusing to a man. When he sees you making decisions with your mother and leaving him out (even though he asked not to be involved), he feels as if this is the prelude of what's to come. He fears that you and your mom will be making decisions for the two of you for the rest of your lives. This makes the professional man worry. Explain to him that this is not reality—this is not how the rest of your life with you as his wife will be. Reassure him that in your long future together all decisions will be made by the two of you.

In spite of all your good intentions, wedding preparations can often turn bloody. Tension will inevitably mount. Fights will break out. They always have, in our experience. In light of this situation, our advice is to keep up the communication between you and your man at all costs. Make time for special dinners or weekends alone with your soon-to-be-husband. We suggest that you keep reminding your family that the wedding is for you and the groom, not for them. It is difficult for a man to tell his fiancée that he would like her to relay this message to her family without insulting her or them. But it's harder for a man not to get upset when a third party gets involved in his and his fiancée's life.

A professional man is used to independence and feeling confident in his abilities. To make your fiancé feel comfortable through this often-stressful time, be gentle when he gets defensive and protective of his individualism. The key phrase that a woman should utter twice a week during this period of planning is, "Everyone needs to understand that *this is our wedding not theirs.*" If you remember this, you will be a success in all phases of this difficult, complicated, exciting time.

So remember, keep your fiancé's feelings in mind—and make sure he knows that you are doing so. He wants you to put him first, not the wedding. Sometimes it seems to the groom that his bride is excited only about the big day—and not their life ahead together. So, be sure to tell your guy how excited you are about your future with him. Always reassure him that the two of you are a team, and no one will come between you.

11

—

THE UGLY TRUTH

We could paint a pretty picture about men—one that you want to see. But we don't think that would be fair—or helpful—to you. We don't believe in sugarcoating our feelings. In order for you to be considered "marriage material" and to get a man to pop the question, you must understand men. The good and the bad. That means the darkness too—the ugly side of our psyches. We want you to know the truth. And if we don't tell you what that is, it is unlikely that you'll hear it from anyone else. So, brace yourself. These six ugly truths may not be what you want to hear, but ultimately they'll help you better understand why we professional men think, act, and work the way we do.

Ugly Truth Number One

Work Takes Precedence Over the Relationship

It's ugly but true. For a man, work is the number-one priority. Number two is you. A man's career affects how he views himself—it's his ego. It's the way in which a man defines himself. It's what he has been working toward his whole life. In many cases, business commitments even take precedence over important family events.

Don't fool yourself. A man is always going to commit to his career before committing to a woman. So a woman should never bother asking a man to choose between her and his career. His choice would clearly be his career.

If Marla had demanded that Rich choose a less-stressful medical field such as dermatology instead of surgery, Rich would've had second thoughts about continuing their relationship. Of course, Marla would never have suggested such a thing since she wants Rich to do what he's passionate about.

In a man's mind his career is truly the heart and soul of his identity.

Ugly Truth Number Two

He's the Star of the Career Show—Like It or Not

In a professional man's eyes, his career is most important. Yes, it is even more important than your career. You could be president of the United States and he could be in his first year at a law firm and, in his mind, your man's job would still be more important than yours is. A man's career is all about ego—it's at work that he competes and performs and is rewarded for his efforts. It is where a man is most comfortable and where he excels. He knows the rules in the business world, and he prides himself in being able to get out there and play with the best of them. To a professional man, his career is what defines him and his life. As far as a man is concerned, his job comes before everything.

Don't misunderstand, we respect a woman's career; men are attracted to independent, intelligent, successful women. And it's not that a man doesn't support his girlfriend's or wife's career or isn't interested in it. Sure, he cares about your career. Of course he wants the best for you. But if he were to choose which is more important—his job or yours—his would win every time. To a man, his career is his top priority.

And we won't stop there. When it comes right down to it, your guy also wants you to acknowledge that his career is more important to your life and your future together than yours is. Men want their egos stroked. If you care about your guy, you should recognize this and be impressed by his achievements, making him feel like number one. You should also make it clear to your man that if it were ever a question of making a sacrifice when it came to work, you would be happy to let a career opportunity go to benefit his professional standing.

The money we earn is nice, but the reason our careers are our focus is that our jobs make us feel good as men. Remember men are very insecure. We want to feel that we are the providers, the heroes, the ones shining with success. Like it or not, in the world in which we live today, a man's professional status carries more importance than that of his wife. There are different criteria for men and women. A man's career is a necessity, but that's not always the case for a woman. When a woman doesn't do well in her career, it's no big deal. When a man doesn't succeed in his career, he's considered a loser. If a woman takes a part-time job, let's say at a drugstore, it's acceptable—she wants to make some extra money. But if a man takes a job at a drugstore, people think that he's unambitious and unsuccessful.

Men define themselves—their whole being—by what they do and by what other people think. Given this, can you blame a man for wanting what he does to be his priority and yours as well?

Ugly Truth Number Three

A Woman Should Never Admit to Having Sex with More Than Ten Men

We don't want to know how many guys you slept with nor do we want to know with whom you slept. A man will break up with an otherwise perfect woman who has "wife potential" simply because she slept with too many guys. Why is this so important to a man? Well, men don't want be associated with a woman who is considered a tramp. Sounds heartless, but that's how it is.

Men can't handle the truth. Certain things are better left unsaid. Too large a number of sexual partners will compel us to break up with you. Our egos won't permit us to live the rest of our lives thinking we have gone where all men have gone before. If your total exceeds ten men, then cap it at ten. You heard us, lie. No man likes to think of his woman sleeping with another guy, much less ten other guys. If your age equals or is less than the number of guys you had sex with, then in a man's eyes, you are practically a prostitute.

Ugly Truth Number Four

If You Want a Man to Marry You, You'd Better Leave Your Baggage at Home in the Closet

When a professional man is looking for a woman with whom to start a life together, the last thing he wants is a woman with baggage. His life is complicated enough as it is. When he is with his girlfriend, he wants to relax, have fun, make love, and enjoy her company. He does not want to play the role of shrink.

Sure, everyone has problems, and relationships are indeed about supporting one another. But if a woman has a ton of problems—and can never seem to deal with them herself—then a man will be turned off. A man likes to feel like a hero and help out from time to time—but he can't save the day every day. Men like independent strong women who aren't needy or full of complaints but instead deal as best they can with their problems. Troubleshooting talks are wonderful—but not for every single conversation.

Ugly Truth Number Five

For Men, the Wedding Is Not Important

Men know that women go gaga over getting married. As far as a man is concerned, the wedding—and everything related to the wedding—is all for you. Men find weddings—even their own—to be not that big a deal. In fact, the wedding is about 10 percent as exciting to your man as it is to you.

First, the proposal. For a man there's a ton of pressure in

buying an engagement ring. Buying an engagement ring is torture—it is an incredibly foreign concept. It's the largest purchase he will make with the least amount of information. It goes against everything a professional man is used to doing—not to mention the expectation of pulling off the most creative proposal in the history of humankind. The pressure for him to do something unique that a woman can brag about to her family and girlfriends is overwhelming.

When it comes to the wedding itself, we know the truth—the wedding is really for the bride. The tune played at almost all weddings is "Here Comes the Bride . . ." The bride is everything. At first, it's a little bit hard for a man to swallow. Sure the day itself is fun—but most men can do without the pomp and circumstance.

Ugly Truth Number Six

Single, Committed, or Married—All Men Are Perverted

Like it or not, your man is thinking about sex all the time, twenty-four hours a day, seven days a week. In fact, the more committed a man is to a woman, the more he fantasizes about other women. Guys are thinking about having sex with other women—be it a waitress, an actress, or a random passerby—all the time. For men, sexual desire is always only slightly beneath the surface.

Men will watch a woman walk by and stare and think about sleeping with her—and her, and her. Men are constantly fantasizing about lesbianism. They're thinking about sleeping with a variety of women. They're dreaming about breasts—or talking about how they're not particularly turned on by breasts. They're worried about the size of their penises. When they're around other men, the locker-room mentality inevitably comes out. Yes, even your boyfriend likes smut. For men it's fun and natural—and nothing for women to get offended by. Why do you think strip clubs, pornographic Web sites, porn magazines, and videos are so successful? Because there's an audience for it—men.

It's true, all men are perverts. Not only do they think about sex, but they enjoy thinking about sex.

So, now you know some ugly truths about men. They may not be things that you hear men talking about on a regular basis—but believe us, they're true. We hope you now have a better understanding of professional men—and the various stages that they go through on the way to commitment. Remember, getting a man to commit is about understanding how your man thinks. Oh, and never, ever pressure him. If you are able to do these things, you'll be a "marriage material" girl in his mind and, before you know it, he'll be popping that question.

AFTERWORD

We have some big news since *Marry Me!* went to press:

Rich married Marla in a lovely ceremony witnessed by two hundred friends and family in Philadelphia. The crowd was touched by the emotional speech Rich made thanking everyone, including the most beautiful woman in the world, Marla, for giving him his most memorable day yet. Brad and Chris, both members of the wedding party, teared up as they congratulated Rich, telling him they had never seen him happier. Rich and Marla spent their first wedded days on a blissful honeymoon in St. Lucia. When they returned, the couple relocated to New York, where Rich took his first job as an orthopedic surgeon at North Star Orthopedics in Forest Hills, New York.

This is just one more piece of evidence that goes to prove that the professional man you have your eye on—or any man you might be dating, no matter what kind of work he does— can commit. Two of us have and we are enjoying married life, just as your man will. Follow our advice and you'll follow your dreams right down the aisle on the arm of the man you love.

For more information please visit our Web site at www.whatmenwant.com.